If You Want Something Done

Center Point
Large Print

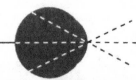

**This Large Print Book carries the
Seal of Approval of N.A.V.H.**

If You Want Something Done

Leadership Lessons from Bold Women

NIKKI R. HALEY

CENTER POINT LARGE PRINT
THORNDIKE, MAINE

To my mom, who taught me how to dream, how to fight, how to love, but most importantly how to live with a faith in God that would get me through anything.

To my daughter, Rena, who gives me hope and inspiration that she is an example of the many amazing women whose stories have yet to be told.

To my sisters, my friends, my heroes, and the women I have yet to meet, it is an honor to share these stories with you.

Contents

Introduction

People matter. Their stories matter.

I decided to write this book because there are incredible women who inspired me throughout my life, and I want other people to be inspired, too. This book is about ten bold and courageous women with ten important lessons to teach us. Of course, they are not the only ten. I chose them because their stories spoke to me, and I found their lessons to be particularly relevant.

Many of these women faced daunting struggles and responsibilities. I talk about my own experiences not to compare but to explain how great leaders can make a difference in our daily lives. From the big decisions to the everyday choices we make, I hope these stories give you the courage to live the life you want and deserve.

Some of the women are living; some come from different historical eras. Some are well known and some less so. Some come from the political realm, and others come from the worlds of athletics and innovation. Some chose their paths in life, and some found themselves, by no choice of their own, facing terrifying choices. They all share something in common that spans time and geography—they embody the qualities that make great leaders. Tenacity. Perseverance.

Service. Decisiveness. Courage. Strength. They made and continue to make an impact on the world. They inspire us, make us want to work harder, be better, do more. Their legacies are not confined to their small or large corner of the universe. Their stories can touch all of us.

Some choices were obvious. In the political realm, Margaret Thatcher has always been a personal hero who inspired me as I ventured into government. Jeane Kirkpatrick was the first female U.S. ambassador to the United Nations, a position I later held. When I came to learn about Golda Meir, one of Israel's founding leaders and its first female prime minister, her story resonated with me, having served as South Carolina's first female executive.

In the human rights realm, I had the privilege of working with Nadia Murad and Cindy Warmbier at the United Nations. They both endured horrible tragedies and showed incredible strength. In the struggle for civil rights, Claudette Colvin and Virginia Walden Ford represent the progress we have made as a country and the ongoing battle to continue that progress.

Finally, Wilma Rudolph, Virginia Hall, and Amelia Earhart were leaders who reached the top of their respective fields. They lived at times when there were low expectations of women professionally, yet they became world class in athletics, espionage, and aviation. They showed the world what is possible when you refuse to give up on your dreams, when you refuse to let adversity define you.

Many of the women in this book were firsts. The first to be prime minister. The first to take a stand. The first to fly. Being the first is hard. It can be lonely and isolating. There is no road map, and people assume something is impossible simply because it hasn't been done before. These women are leaders because they paved the way for the women who came after them. We walk in their footsteps and leave a well-trodden path for the women who come after us.

As you read these pages, remember we have the potential to make life better for others. In our own small way, we can inspire, mentor, and encourage other women to do great things. So, don't hold back. Don't be silent. Don't give in to fear.

Be bold. Be adventurous. Be yourself. There will always be people who want to tell you what you can do and what you can't. What is possible and what is not. I know because I have encountered those people throughout my life. Some of them were well meaning. But all of them wanted to limit my potential. Your potential is limitless. Your life—the life you want—is worth fighting for.

So, fight.

1

It's easy to talk about principles. It's hard to stand by them when everyone is lined up against you. No one embodied this truth better than Margaret Thatcher, Britain's first female prime minister. She wanted to save Great Britain, and she knew it would be difficult. That didn't stop her. That was a reason to forge ahead. That's why she's always been an inspiration to me. And that's why I borrowed a version of her famous quote for the title of this book.

"If you want something said, ask a man. If you want something done, ask a woman." Margaret Thatcher didn't want to become prime minister to sit around and talk. She wanted to do things. Big things. Important things. This determination in the face of opposition defines many of the women in this book. It was how my mother raised us—to confront problems head-on and find solutions. And it struck a chord with me as I sought to leave my mark on South Carolina.

I ran for office to make a difference. I've always believed the best way to appreciate God's blessings is to give back. But to really work to lift up everyone and make lives better, you have to be willing to shake things up.

The best—or worst—example of this was my

fight against the practice of holding voice votes and not showing individual votes on the record in the South Carolina state legislature. If you wanted to see how your legislator voted on an important bill—like voting for a pay increase for themselves—you couldn't look it up. There was no record. There was no transparency and no way to hold legislators accountable. It was embarrassing, and it had to stop.

I wrote a bill that would require a roll call vote on any legislation that spent or raised taxpayer money. Only one other legislator wanted to sponsor the bill. At a Republican meeting, the Speaker of the House attacked me for daring to challenge how the legislature had long operated. He actually said they would decide what voters needed to see and what they didn't.

I was appalled and frustrated. I knew the people of South Carolina would agree with me if they knew what was happening, so I took the fight to them. I traveled around the state urging voters to call their legislators and tell them to support my bill that simply stated anything important enough to be debated on the floor of the House or Senate should require a legislative vote on the record. This made my Republican leaders furious—so furious that the Speaker stripped me of all my positions. He wanted to make an example of me, as if to say, "This is what happens when you challenge the establishment."

If that was supposed to dissuade me, it failed. His retaliation only made me want to succeed more. I went to the press and told my side of the story. This fight coincided with the rise of the Tea Party movement, and thousands of people all across South Carolina joined the fight for accountability.

When the legislature blackballed me for my fight, I did the only thing left I knew to do. I ran for governor. After I became governor, it was one of the first bills I signed into law. The day of the signing ceremony, we blasted Pat Benatar's "Hit Me with Your Best Shot" from the sound system in the statehouse. The establishment certainly tried to hit me with its best shot. It failed. Now in South Carolina, every legislator has to show their vote on the record, and we took it a step further—including their spending on every section of the budget.

That fight hurt, but I learned a lot from it. When you try to make a difference, there are always going to be people who want to stop you. My fellow legislators certainly enjoyed the system of zero transparency, and they fought back with everything they had to humiliate me. They threatened me, they punished me, and they tried to shame me. You have to be willing to put it all on the line. And you have to be willing to go through the pain to do what is right.

Margaret Thatcher was better at this than

anyone. She took on fights no one thought she could win—and she won many of them. She wasn't an obvious choice for leader of Britain's Conservative Party. She was a grocer's daughter and a woman. There were few people who looked like her or shared her middle-class background in British politics. Her Tory Party was dominated by upper-class men who were used to getting their way. She went into the thick of battle knowing she would be dismissed and attacked, and she used that to her advantage. She saved Britain from socialist collapse, inspired countless conservatives, and made history. Not bad for "the Grocer's Daughter"—one of the many nicknames given to her by her opponents. Not bad at all.

Margaret Thatcher

Stand for Principle

If you want something said, ask a man. If you want something done, ask a woman.

—MARGARET THATCHER

I wear heels. It's not for a fashion statement. It's because if I see something wrong, we're going to kick 'em every single time.[1]

—NIKKI HALEY

On January 19, 1976, Margaret Thatcher gave a speech that would define her leadership and her legacy. The speech focused on her recent trip to West Germany, where she visited British armed forces. She called for investing in the British military as the world grappled with Soviet Communism. The Marxists, she argued, were "bent on world dominance," and Britain was ill prepared to meet the challenge of the moment. This particular challenge demanded a reckoning: "This was a moment when our choice will determine the life or death of our kind of society: Let's ensure that our children will have cause to rejoice that we did not forsake their freedom."[2]

It was a good speech but not a revolutionary one. Thatcher hit on many of the same themes she had been trumpeting since she became the Tory Party's opposition leader in 1975. But she got lucky. The Soviet Union's military newspaper, the *Red Star*, criticized her speech by comparing her to Germany's Otto von Bismarck, the nineteenth-century "Iron Chancellor." The insult of choice? The Soviets called her the "Iron Lady."[3]

Thatcher embraced the insult as a badge of honor. Shortly after the article was published, she introduced herself to the Conservative Association of Finchley, saying, "I stand before you tonight in my Red Star chiffon evening gown, my face softly made up and my fair hair gently waved, the Iron Lady of the Western world. A Cold War warrior. . . . Yes, I am an iron lady . . . if that's how they wish to interpret my defense of values and freedoms fundamental to our way of life."[4]

Where did her iron will come from? It came from a passionate love of country and the belief that Britain was repeatedly let down and humiliated by its leaders. It came from watching Britain go from being a world superpower to being "the sick man of Europe."[5] It came from a fierce sense of principle and the confidence that she was right. And it came with time, practice, and experience—decades of being dismissed strengthened her backbone. She developed an immunity to the outrage of the chattering class.

Margaret Thatcher shaped Britain, and Britain shaped her. As she climbed the ranks of government in the second half of the twentieth century, she watched socialism destroy England's economy and standing in the world. And she watched England withdraw from international affairs as the United States and Soviet Union dominated the world stage.

Ted Heath, her predecessor as Conservative leader, won election in 1970 on a free-market agenda, but he quickly caved when the economy took a turn for the worse. Under Heath, the government printed money to fuel its spending increases, bailed out failing industries, and introduced wage and price controls.[6] When Heath called an election in 1974 under the slogan "Who Governs Britain?" the British people responded by handing the socialist Labour Party a resounding victory.[7]

For Thatcher, Conservative defeat in 1974 was a turning point. She viewed Ted Heath's political rout as a public rebuke of the party's lukewarm philosophy. Conservatives wasted their majority on consensus—a word Margaret hated with every bone in her body.[8] "The Old Testament prophets didn't go out into the highways saying, 'Brothers, I want consensus,'" she remarked. "They said, 'this is my faith and my vision. This is what I passionately believe.' And they preached it."[9]

By the time Thatcher became opposition leader in 1975, Britain was in a sorry state. Inflation would soar to a record-breaking 25 percent that year.[10] The government owned or controlled more than half of the country's economic output.[11] The once-mighty Britain was trapped in a cycle of government spending and taxation.

Her years as opposition leader gave Thatcher an opportunity to take her faith and vision for a test drive. It began by staking out unchartered ground on the most important issue facing Britain and the world: Soviet Communism. Thatcher's rejection of socialism and communism wasn't just economic. It was a moral crusade against an existential threat. Communism denied people their God-given rights to freedom. Therefore, it had to be eradicated. This was not a popular opinion in the Tory Party or even in much of the Western world. Under U.S. president Richard Nixon, the 1970s was defined by a policy of détente—an easing of hostilities between America and the Soviet Union and a commitment to working with each other.[12]

Her view of socialism at home wasn't that different. She believed it was a moral crime for government to strip people of their right to make economic choices, to own property, and to build better lives for themselves and their families. She lambasted socialism's insistence on equality of results in a speech called "Let

Our Children Grow Tall." The punch line was: "Let our children grow tall and some taller than others if they have the ability to do so."[13] When she spoke of England's economic hardship, she didn't talk about statistics and numbers. She spoke in big, bold declarations. "Inflation," she declared during her inaugural trip to America, "is a pernicious evil capable of destroying any society built on a value system where freedom is paramount."[14]

Back home, the liberal newspaper *The Guardian* wrote a scathing but not inaccurate review of her trip to the States. "Mrs. Thatcher's speeches . . . show that she has broken decisively with the Disraelian Tory tradition of pragmatism." *The Guardian* was right. Pragmatism . . . consensus . . . Thatcher believed these timid words held Britain back from realizing its potential. "It is often said that politics is the art of the possible," she said. "The danger of such a phrase is that we may deem impossible things which would be possible, indeed desirable, if only we had more courage, more insight."[15]

It was this insistence on a courageous, ideological vision that shepherded Margaret Thatcher into power. It helped that the ruling Labour Party had thrown the British economy into a tailspin.

The winter of 1978/79 was England's coldest winter in sixteen years.[16] The weather matched the mood of the country. Britain was beaten down by record-breaking inflation and a crippling industrial crisis. Worker strikes plagued nearly every sector of the economy. From bread strikes to hospital strikes to trucking strikes to sanitation strikes, millions of people stopped doing their jobs. Trains didn't run, packages weren't delivered, garbage piled up in the street, and unburied bodies filled graveyards. This period became known as the "Winter of Discontent."[17] In classic British fashion, it was a massive understatement.

On January 10, 1979, Labour Party prime minister James Callaghan gave a press conference upon returning from an official trip overseas. When asked to respond to criticism that he shouldn't have traveled during this time of economic turmoil, his dismissive answer resulted in a devastating headline.[18]

The next morning, *The Sun* declared, CRISIS? WHAT CRISIS? These words sounded Labour's death knell.[19] On March 28, 1979, the incumbent government lost a no-confidence vote by a single vote, forcing an election.[20]

On May 4, 1979, Margaret Thatcher made history. Conservatives claimed a forty-three-seat majority, and Thatcher was elected prime minister.[21] It was a crowning achievement at a time when few women occupied the heights of political power. But it was also a sobering moment. Britain's past and future were colliding, and it was up to her to chart the course.

It was not a course for the faint of heart. Thatcher broke ranks with decades of Keynesian economics, which demanded more government spending. Thatcher subscribed to monetarism—a theory embraced by Milton Friedman and other free-market thinkers who believed the amount of money in supply was directly responsible for inflation. Too much money in circulation depressed the value of the British pound. If Thatcher wanted to curb inflation, she'd have to get the money supply under control. She started by cutting government spending, increasing interest rates, cutting income taxes, and increasing the value-added tax (Europe's version of a sales tax).[22]

As 1979 turned into 1980, Thatcher's austerity measures exacted more pain from the British people. Inflation wouldn't begin to drop until 1981. In the meantime, unemployment rose quickly, and gross domestic product dropped just as fast. By the time Margaret Thatcher delivered her second conference speech as prime minister in October 1980, she had a recession on her hands.[23]

The pressure mounted for Thatcher to reverse course, or pull what the media dubbed a "U-turn." After all, that's exactly what Ted Heath had done. Now the Heath wing of the Tory Party—known as the "Wets"—and the liberal Labour Party were calling for a reversal, along with a throng of economists, the media, and members of her own cabinet.[24]

The environment had all the makings of a pressure cooker. So many people were rooting for Thatcher to fail. Could the Iron Lady withstand the tension?

October 10, 1980, was a stormy day, and the icy rain was unforgiving. That didn't stop 4,000 protestors from gathering outside the conference center and yelling, "Maggie, Maggie, out, out, out!" It took 2,500 police officers to contain the crowd.[25]

Inside, Thatcher prepared to give her speech to the rank-and-file members of the Conservative Party. But it wasn't just the party faithful she was speaking to. The eyes of the country—and the world—were upon her.

On that rainy October day, Margaret Thatcher had a choice. It was not an obvious choice. Millions of people were hurting. Many in her own party didn't have her back. Many suspected she wasn't cut out for leadership simply because she was a woman. They viewed the economic chaos as confirmation of their suspicions.

But they underestimated her. They didn't know her—and those who did didn't understand her. Few recalled or even knew that her crusade to save Britain was decades in the making. Thirty years prior, when she was only twenty-four years old, she made her first political run for Parliament in the working-class area of Dartford. She made her pitch to voters in a newspaper article, offering them a choice between Britain as it was and Britain as it was meant to be.[26]

> Are YOU going to let this proud island race, who at one time would never accept charity, drift on from crisis to crisis under a further spell of shaky Socialist finance? Or do you believe in sound finance and economical spending of public money, such as the Conservatives will adopt? YOU will decide. . . . Do you want it to perish for a soul-less Socialist system, or to live to recreate a glorious Britain? YOU WILL DECIDE.[27]

The choice in 1980 was the same as it had been thirty years before. The only difference was *she* was in charge. The protestors were chanting *her* name. The TV cameras were zoomed in on *her* face. The world was listening to *her* words.

She began her speech by acknowledging the challenge at hand. It was no small thing to reverse four decades of economic sickness and national decline. She acknowledged the pain caused by unemployment. She didn't try to spin the numbers and make them look better than they were.[28]

But she also highlighted everything Conservatives had accomplished in seventeen months. They were opening up the British economy to competition, they had begun the difficult task of cracking the whip on trade unions, they eliminated exchange controls that prohibited foreign investment, they introduced important reforms to reduce government monopolies, and they began the process of selling off council homes—Britain's version of public housing.[29]

Then she turned to her critics and declared, "To those waiting with bated breath for that favourite media catchphrase, the 'U' turn, I have only one thing to say. 'You turn if you want to. The lady's not for turning.' "[30]

The soon-to-be famous line was a spoof on a play by Christopher Fry called *The Lady's Not for Burning*.[31] Few people remember the source. But many remember Thatcher's defiant declaration, a reminder that she was not the typical politician who turned back the minute the going got tough. It was a reminder that she was indeed the Iron Lady.

That 1980 speech was a big test, but the pressure to perform a U-turn continued throughout Thatcher's premiership. In 1982, as unemployment hovered at 13 percent, she responded to the pressure with a new slogan—"The Resolute Approach." The three words hung on a banner when she gave her third conference speech: "We will not disguise our purpose nor betray our principles. We will do what must be done. We will tell the people the truth and the people will be our judge."[32]

Thatcher's refusal to do a U-turn was important for two reasons. First, her economic policies kick-started the change Britain needed. Over ten years in office, Thatcher reversed forty years of socialism. She privatized major industries and utilities, including British Telecom, British Gas, British Steel, British Petroleum, British Airways, Jaguar, Rolls-Royce, and the water and electricity utilities.[33] She took on the powerful trade unions, passing legislation that removed their legal immunity and making them financially liable for damages.[34] She brought inflation down, cut the top income tax rate from 98 percent to 40 percent, deregulated the financial sector, and helped turn London into a financial powerhouse.[35] She also became increasingly opposed to efforts to erode Britain's economic independence in favor of a European collective.[36]

The second reason goes back to Margaret Thatcher's initial diagnosis when she was an aspiring member of Parliament, all of twenty-four years old. Thatcher believed—correctly— that the British people were tired of weak-kneed leaders. They were tired of being laughed at and discounted. They were desperate for a leader who believed in Britain enough to fight for it. That fighter was Margaret Thatcher. Her confidence and faith were contagious. Her strength was Britain's strength.

Thatcher's appeal wasn't just ideological. It was emotional. She taught Britain to believe in itself again. She reminded people that they didn't have to settle, that it's okay to dream and to stand by that dream when people tell you it can't be done.

What was the secret to her success? She believed in Britain, but more importantly, she believed in herself. As a female politician, she was used to being dismissed, criticized, and picked apart. She was too female, too principled, too demanding. Her voice was "too shrill," her clothing "too fussy."[37] She earned a slew of nasty nicknames, from "Thatcher, the Milksnatcher"[38] to "Attila the Hen"[39] to "T.B.W.—That Bloody Woman."[40]

There is a long list of people who thought she wouldn't go far. Upon meeting her in 1975, Henry Kissinger remarked, "I don't think Margaret Thatcher will last."[41] Even Milton Friedman, whom Thatcher admired, wrote, "She is a very attractive and interesting lady. Whether she really has the capacities that Britain so badly needs at this time, I must confess, seems to me a very open question."[42]

At home, she had many detractors. Some were

downright sexist. It was not unusual for her fellow members of Parliament to catcall when she spoke.[43] When she ran for opposition leader, *The Economist* described her as "precisely the sort of candidate who ought to be able to stand, and lose, harmlessly." Others were more dismissive: "We don't need to take this Thatcher business seriously, do we?"[44] Even when she won, the press asked her what issue propelled her to victory. She responded, "I like to think it was merit." "Could you expand on that?" they pressed. She didn't take the bait. "No, it doesn't need expansion."[45]

Margaret Thatcher died in 2013, but she is still loved and hated, admired and denounced. Her famous quips are still repeated and quoted. Her story lives on. She is larger than life because she embodied what so many of us want to be: confident, courageous, principled. Those are simple things, but sometimes the simplest things are the hardest.

In a public eye where everything you say and believe is scrutinized under a microscope, believing in yourself and standing by your principles are more important than ever. The internet and social media make every John Doe an expert and a critic. The bigger and bolder the idea, the harsher and louder the criticism. It can be tempting to sit on the sidelines and let the world pass you by.

With that attitude, there never would have been a Margaret Thatcher or an Iron Lady. Britain might still be "the sick man of Europe." Standing for principle takes courage—courage to put yourself out there in the first place, courage to stand tall when others try to knock you down, courage to see your vision through, no matter how long it takes. Refusing to try, failing to dream, would be the biggest tragedy of all.

Margaret Thatcher was a fighter, and she relished the fight. She understood that change doesn't happen without pushing people, making them uncomfortable, and yes, making them angry. An eager student of literature, she kept a copy of "No Enemies" by the Scottish poet Charles Mackay nearby to lift her spirits during her more contentious moments. It reads, "You have no enemies, you say? / Alas! my friend, the boast is poor; / He who has mingled in the fray / Of duty, that the brave endure, / Must have made foes! If you have none, / Small is the work that you have done. . . . [You've never turned the wrong to right, / You've been a coward in the fight.]"

When you find yourself at a crossroads, staring down the barrel of a choice between principle and popular opinion, ask yourself, What would the Iron Lady do? I'm willing to bet she would hold her head high and march on. She might—if she could spare a moment—destroy her opponents with a devastating one-liner. One thing she would not do is retreat.

Don't shy away from the fight because it might be hard. Know that it *will* be hard. The best fights, the best ideas, are hard. They are also the most worthwhile.

2

When I first stepped foot in the United Nations in the winter of 2017, it reminded me of high school. The cliques, the rumors, the popular kids and the loners, the bullies and the bullied.

I knew from the beginning that I didn't care if I was liked. After all, I didn't agree to be President Trump's ambassador to the United Nations to make friends. I had a job to do, and what an awesome job it was. It was the opportunity of a lifetime to defend the country I love so much. My goal was to make sure countries knew what America was for and what we were against. I came to the United Nations to make sure the United States was respected, to have the backs of our friends, and to stand up to our enemies. I didn't want there to be any gray in my communication.

Although I didn't have a typical résumé for the job of ambassador, I had one thing going for me: I was used to being an outsider. Growing up in Bamberg, South Carolina, I was a brown girl in a black-and-white world. We were the only Indian family in a small Southern town. Our neighbors didn't know who we were, what we were, or why we were there. That changed over time, but I would continue to play the role of outsider throughout my life. From the Old Boys Club at the state legislature to serving as South Carolina's first female and minority governor, I was used to the question marks on people's faces that said, "What is she doing here?"

A lot had changed since the 1980s, when Jeane Kirkpatrick became America's first female ambassador to the United Nations, but not enough. For many of my fellow ambassadors, it was odd to see a woman in a position of power. In 2017, there was one female on the fifteen-member UN Security Council—me. More than that, it was odd to see an outspoken woman who didn't defer and cave. After eight years of President Obama's weakness, my colleagues were not used to seeing America stand up for itself. Too many people expected America—and me—to go along and get along.

That's never been me, and that should never be America.

It was encouraging to know Jeane Kirkpatrick had walked this same ground three decades prior as Ronald Reagan's ambassador to the United Nations and a member of his National Security Council (NSC). She was America's first female UN ambassador and the only woman on the NSC. Like me, she didn't come from a traditional diplomatic background. She didn't fit the mold of what people expected. And she didn't care about being liked.

Jeane Kirkpatrick was a lot of things—smart, determined, passionate—but the quality that defined her time at the United Nations was her refusal to apologize. Apologize for what? For speaking her mind and the truth, for being a proud American, for promoting freedom. Whether she was defending Israel, denouncing the Soviet Union, or calling out the United Nations's hypocrisy, Jeane spoke with the pride of someone who knew she stood on the right side of history.

It wasn't easy. Jeane never thought of herself as a fighter. "I am not someone who is personally tough," she said in 1981.[1] She was a professor and an academic by training. She wasn't schooled in the art of politics or navigating bureaucratic red tape. She didn't relish her fights with Secretary of State Alexander Haig or the dirty whispers behind her back by the Soviet propaganda machine.

Sometimes she questioned why she put up with it—but the answer was always the same: "I think it's my duty. I have a demanding conception of citizenship. I have an obligation to confront serious problems."[2] She believed her words mattered. Fighting for freedom mattered. Defending Israel from the hypocritical, anti-Semitic UN mattered. Dismantling Communism mattered. Giving a voice to the thousands of dissidents locked behind bars mattered. Broadcasting American pride and strength mattered.

She was reminded just how much her work mattered on a trip to the Soviet Union. Andrei Sakharov, a renowned physicist and Soviet dissident, approached her and declared, "Kirkpatski, Kirkpatski. I have so wanted to meet you and thank you in person. Your name is known in all the Gulag."[3]

The *Gulag* was the acronym for the Soviet agency overseeing the network of labor camps that became known simply as the *gulags*. Life in the gulags was brutal.[4] The men and women there had little rest from the forced labor, starvation, and illness that plagued the camps. But Jeane Kirkpatrick gave them something else. She gave them hope.

After four years of President Jimmy Carter's failed administration, the world saw America as weak because we saw ourselves as weak. We didn't stand up to our enemies, and we certainly didn't have the backs of our friends. All that changed when Jeane Kirkpatrick arrived on the scene. Our enemies took notice, but more importantly, our allies took notice, too. For the millions of people subjugated under the Soviet Union's Iron Curtain, American strength bred hope. Hope for freedom. Hope for dignity. Hope for change. In 1981, thirty-six years into the Cold War, the world desperately needed more of all of the above.

Jeane Kirkpatrick knew the power of her voice and used it unapologetically. She's a reminder to all of us not to ever stop using the power of our voices.

Jeane Kirkpatrick

Don't Apologize

The enterprise [the Security Council] more closely resembles a mugging than either a political debate or an effort at problem-solving.[5]
—AMBASSADOR JEANE KIRKPATRICK

With all due respect, I don't get confused.[6]
—AMBASSADOR NIKKI HALEY

Jeane Kirkpatrick was an outsider in every sense.

For starters, she was a Democrat in a Republican administration. She was a woman in politics when few women ventured into the political muck. She was a diplomat without diplomatic experience. She was a person of principle who refused to bend to and abide by the status quo. And she was an outspoken fighter in an arena that expected her to shut up.

Well, the United Nations had the wrong woman. If there was one thing Jeane Kirkpatrick would not do, it was shut up. "I do not leave important things unsaid," she told a reporter from *The Boston Globe*.[7] And that's why Ronald Reagan chose her to be his permanent representative to the United Nations in early 1981.

She didn't know what to expect when she assumed the role, though she was not naïve. She had watched previous ambassadors like Daniel Patrick Moynihan battle pervasive anti-Americanism and anti-Semitism just a few years earlier.[8] She remembered Adlai Stevenson boldly demanding answers from his Soviet counterpart during the Cuban missile crisis.[9]

She was prepared to do battle with the Soviet Union and the Arab bloc, among others, but she didn't expect to do battle with her American colleagues back in Washington. They were supposed to be on the same side—the side of freedom, human rights, democracy. Or so she thought. Throughout her four years at the United Nations, Jeane butted heads repeatedly with the State Department, especially Reagan's first secretary of state, Alexander Haig.

The institutionalists at the State Department wanted one thing: not to rock the boat. They saw stability as good and change as bad. They had grown accustomed to being a doormat for the world's thugs and dictators, and they had no intention of changing course.

Unfortunately for them, Jeane had every intention of changing course. Ronald Reagan credited her with taking the "Kick Me" sign off the United States' back.[10] She refused to cower in the face of evil. She refused to apologize for standing up for human rights and democracy. She refused to be bullied. While the American media portrayed her as a right-wing idealogue[11] (she was still a registered Democrat), she was neither strident nor tactless. She simply knew what was at stake.

All this came to a head in her third year at the United Nations. Nineteen eighty-three was a scary time. The United States and the Soviet Union seemed destined for an explosive collision. In March, President Reagan declared the Soviet Union an "evil empire" and proposed a missile defense system that his critics mocked as "Star Wars." The Cold War grew increasingly hot. Everyone was on edge.[12]

Then, on September 1, 1983, a South Korean airliner was shot out of the sky and fell into the Sea of Japan. All 269 passengers and crew members were killed. It didn't take long for the world to determine what happened and who did it. The question was why.[13]

Korean Air Lines Flight 007 (KAL 007) was on the last leg of its flight from New York City to Seoul with a stopover in Anchorage, Alaska, when it veered off course and ventured into Soviet airspace. The Boeing jet flew two and a half hours over Russian airspace and was just two minutes from leaving it when a Soviet fighter jet shot it down.[14]

At the time, Jeane and her husband were in Morocco visiting King Hassan II, and she saw no reason to cut her trip short. But it soon became clear that this was no accident. Thanks to Japanese listening devices, America had access to radio transmission recordings between Soviet ground control and its pilots. The conversation was damning.[15]

The U.S. government deduced several things from the recording. One, the attack was deliberate. Two, it was premeditated. Three, the Russian pilots were able to see the airliner and its identifying symbols.[16] And yet, the Soviet government refused to admit responsibility. Indeed, it took five days for Russia to even acknowledge that the Korean plane disappeared above its waters.[17] (It would take eight years for the Soviet Union to issue a formal apology for the attack.[18])

On September 5, President Reagan addressed the American people on national TV. He did not mince words. He called the incident a "massacre," an "attack by the Soviet Union," and a "crime against humanity."[19] Still, Reagan's harsh charges were moderate compared to what was to come.

One day later, on September 6, Jeane Kirkpatrick gave a speech at the UN Security Council that reverberated around the world. She spoke with a conviction and moral clarity that was so rarely seen at the United Nations. But that was not the only unusual thing that day.

Kirkpatrick's team asked the United Nations to hook up four video monitors in the Security Council chamber—something that had never been done before—so she could play a ten-minute tape of the radio transmission recording with English subtitles. The bureaucrats at the United Nations were reluctant, but Jeane's team prevailed on them. One hurdle down.[20]

This historic moment was almost over before it began. Scheduled to speak at 10:00 a.m., Jeane paced the large Security Council room waiting for the tape to arrive. But the staffers bringing the tape from Washington, D.C., to New York City were stranded at LaGuardia Airport waiting for their car, which had been mistakenly taken by Kirkpatrick's legal counsel. It all worked out when they hopped in a taxi, zigzagged through New York City traffic, and delivered the tape at 10:20 a.m.[21]

It was the kind of comedy of errors one can look back at and laugh. But as the minutes ticked by, it was no laughing matter. Jeane knew she couldn't speak without the tape. The world needed to see and hear the evidence.

Jeane rose to speak. Like a prosecutor on the attack, she organized her arguments logically, knocking down the Soviets' excuses one by one. She argued that the Soviet Union had repeatedly lied about the facts of the attack, claiming it thought it was shooting down a U.S. reconnaissance plane, that it was the airliner's fault for flying through Soviet airspace in the first place, that the Americans were making a "hullabaloo" over nothing.[22] She prepped her audience for what they would hear on the recording. Then she introduced the tape.

> Soviet SU-15 (805) at 1818:34 GMT: The A.N.O. [air navigation lights] are burning. The strobe light is flashing.
> MiG-23 (163) at 1818:56 GMT: Roger, I'm at 7500, course 230.
> SU-15 (805) at 1819:02 GMT: I am closing on the target.
> SU-15 (805) at 1826:20 GMT: I have executed the launch.
> SU-15 (805) at 1826:22 GMT: The target is destroyed.
> SU-15 (805) at 1826:27 GMT: I am breaking off attack.[23]

The video, she explained, showed that the Soviet pilots saw KAL 007 for at least twenty minutes before firing. Contrary to Soviet claims, the Soviet pilots did not try to communicate with the Korean pilots or question KAL 007's identity, whether it was civilian or military. The pilots did not mention firing warning shots.[24]

Then she asked the big question: Why did the Soviets shoot the plane down when it had only two minutes to go before leaving Russian airspace? Her answer was unequivocal:

> The fact is that violence and lies are regular instruments of Soviet policy. . . . Whether the destruction of K.A.L. 7 and its passengers reflect only utter indifference to human life, or whether that destruction was designed to intimidate, we are dealing here not with pilot error but with decisions and priorities characteristic of a system. . . . We are reminded once again that the Soviet Union is a state based on the dual principles of callousness and mendacity, dedicated to the rule of force. . . . It is this principle of force, this mentality of force, that lies at the root of the Korean Air Line tragedy.[25]

Years of academic research had prepared Kirkpatrick for this moment. Thanks to her professors at Barnard and Columbia, and later, her job at the State Department, she had access to internal Nazi and Soviet documents detailing the systematic oppression that buttressed those regimes. She dedicated her career to studying the nature and rise of totalitarianism.[26] And now she occupied the biggest stage in the world to share what she had learned.

The Soviet Union wasn't just a bad regime, run by bad guys. Soviet Communism was an evil ideology with no respect for human life, international norms, or common decency. The "evil empire" could not be pushed gradually toward democracy or reformed. The rot was endemic to the regime. That was the real lesson of the KAL 007 tragedy.

What was the result of Jeane's speech? For six more days, the UN Security Council debated and rehashed the KAL 007 tragedy, leading up to a vote on a resolution condemning the Soviet attack. Everyone expected Russia to veto the resolution if given the chance, but the United States needed to muster nine votes to adopt the resolution and force the Soviet veto.[27]

Even this minor step seemed too great a hurdle for the United Nations.

The United States could depend on France, the United Kingdom, the Netherlands, Pakistan, Togo, Jordan, and Zaire to vote for the resolution. Kirkpatrick's team turned its attention to Zimbabwe and Malta. Zimbabwe was a no-go. Its dictator, Robert Mugabe, had no interest in opposing the Soviet Union. Efforts to woo Malta quickly fell apart, too. It was only after some last-minute dealmaking—minutes before the vote took place—that Malta agreed to vote yes. The resolution had its nine votes. It was the first time in four years that the UN Security Council was able to adopt a resolution critical of the Soviet Union.[28]

Yes, Russia quickly vetoed the resolution. Yes, the resolution was weak by American standards, having been watered down to attract enough votes.[29] The cynics could question the point of the entire exercise. What did the United States gain?

The small victory unleashed real-world shifts in international relations. Immediately following the veto, Japan launched sanctions on the Russian airline Aeroflot. A majority of NATO members suspended air traffic with the Soviet Union for two weeks. The International Federation of Airline Pilots' Associations instituted a sixty-day ban on flights to the Soviet Union.[30]

But it was more than that. The Cold War was a power struggle—and not just between the United States and the Soviet Union or the West and the East. This was an age-old battle between good and evil, democracy and tyranny. For too long, the world's nations cowered at the Soviet Union's feet on matters big and small. From its invasion of Afghanistan to its allegiance with the Arab bloc on all things Israel related to its support for Communist Cuba and Nicaragua, the Soviet Union was the proverbial Goliath at the United Nations. And for too long, the

United States had acted like David without the courage.

This backdrop set the stage for a showdown in the early days of September 1983. For the first time in a long time, America won a moral victory on the global stage. The world watched and took notes. They saw a strong America standing up for human rights. They saw a weakened Soviet Union ashamed and chastised.

It was a big deal.

Jeane could have taken the easy way out. She could have given a perfunctory speech—like the State Department's official statement denouncing the "competence of the Soviet air defense system"[31]—and called it a day, chalking up defeat to business as usual at the United Nations. She could have given the speech and not gone the extra mile to convince the United Nations to hook up the TV monitors in the Security Council chamber. She could have given up when the United States and its allies didn't have the nine votes needed to adopt the anti-Soviet resolution. She could have—but she didn't.

We live in a time when we are expected to apologize for everything—as individuals and as a nation. Cancel culture demands ideological conformity by squeezing apologies out of people who dare to disagree with woke orthodoxy. Everyone, everything is scrutinized and judged—what we say, what we believe, the books we read, the shows we watch, even the historical figures we choose to honor.

An entire philosophy has emerged around the ridiculous idea that America is inherently evil and we must constantly atone for our collective sins. This national self-loathing permeates our lives. In school, young children are taught to feel guilty for being American. In corporate America and even the halls of our government, workers are forced to undergo "training" sessions to correct their "privileged" misconceptions. In this new woke religion, we are all tainted by America's original sin. Moral redemption is only possible through our public mea culpas.

This woke madness is new, but its seeds took root during Jeane Kirkpatrick's political conversion. It was the same kind of self-hatred and self-righteous guilt that soured Jeane on the Democratic Party in the 1960s and 1970s. A proud Democrat for most of her life, she couldn't stomach the Left's obsession with anti-Americanism.[32] This disgust propelled her to accept a job in the Reagan administration. It fueled her fire when she stood up to the apologists at the State Department and the anti-American bullies at the United Nations. And it pushed her to do something else she never thought she would do.

In 1984, Jeane pulled off the Band-Aid and declared herself a Republican at the Republican

National Convention. The former Democrat was the star of the show. The Democratic Party of her youth was very different from the Democrats of 1984. Today's Democrats, she said, "behaved less like a dove or a hawk than like an ostrich—convinced it would shut out the world by hiding its head in the sand."[33]

American greatness derives from and depends on its strength. Great leaders of all political stripes, she continued, "were not afraid to be resolute nor ashamed to speak of America as a great nation." In contrast, an apologetic foreign policy came at great cost. Under Carter, the world witnessed a wave of totalitarian triumphs. From the fall of Saigon to the Soviet Union's invasion of Afghanistan to Ayatollah Khomeini's rise in Iran to the Sandinistas' one-party rule in Nicaragua, Carter represented an era of weakness and retreat, led by people who, as Kirkpatrick said, "always blame America first."[34]

Ronald Reagan's election in 1980, along with Jeane Kirkpatrick's tenure at the United Nations, marked a new era in America. As Reagan declared in his 1984 reelection ad, it was "morning again in America."[35] It wasn't just a policy shift. It was an existential shift, a change in the way Americans viewed themselves.

Standing up for ourselves and our country starts with the conviction that we are worth standing up for. This is true in politics and life. Whether we are standing up to Communist China or the woke mobs at our schools, whether we are taking on a school bully or the "mean girls" of Twitter, take this message to heart. We have nothing to apologize for.

On the contrary, we have so much to be proud of. Use the power of your voice to remind everyone that even on our worst day, we are blessed to live in America.

3

My parents taught my siblings and me one lesson that always stuck with me: don't complain about it; do something about it. It is wasted energy to complain about something. The best thing you can do is put that same energy into fixing the problem.

My parents embodied this lesson. They left well-to-do lifestyles in India in search of a better life for themselves and their growing family. My mom was a lawyer and was appointed one of the first female judges in India, but due to the challenges facing women at the time, she was unable to serve on the bench. They didn't settle for the life they had. They changed their circumstances to make it better.

I started doing the books for my family's business when I was thirteen. It wasn't until I got to college that I realized that wasn't normal! I went on to graduate from college with a degree in accounting. After working in the corporate world, I was tired of working for the guys down the hall and came back home to work in our family's business.

Small businesses are the backbone of our country, and there is never a day that's easy. One morning, I was having a conversation with my mom about how hard it was to make a dollar and how easy it was for government to take it. She followed up with that familiar reminder, "Don't complain about it. Do something about it."

Ignorance is bliss. I ended up running in a Republican primary against the longest-serving legislator in South Carolina. Once I got into the race, I realized how popular he was. It seemed like he was related to half the district. He was an example of the old boys club. He once said, "Women are best suited for secretarial work, decorating cakes, and counter sales, like selling lingerie." Let that one sink in a bit.

There were a lot of strikes against me. I was young. I was female. I was Indian. And I was relatively unknown. However, I have always had a great work ethic and, more importantly, a passion to fight for what I believe is right.

Losing was not an option. My husband, Michael, got into the driver's seat, I was in the passenger seat, we put our two little ones in the back seat, and I started knocking on doors. When I met people, I said no disrespect to the incumbent, but we had way too many lawyers in the statehouse, and I believed they needed a really good accountant.

Shortly before the election, my opponent dropped a mailer across the district that was a comparison piece. On one side was his face and the words *white male, Christian, business owner.*

Then there was a picture of me and the words *Indian female, Buddhist* (a lie), *housekeeper* (another lie). He knew how damaging a piece like that would be in a Southern district.

I had converted to Christianity when Michael and I were married. Both of our children were baptized. I had no problem talking about my faith, but this wasn't an honest conversation. This was an underhanded effort to spread lies about my background and inflame people's worst instincts against me. That wasn't the end of it. Then he ran a half-page ad that went out of its way to refer to me as "Nimrata N. Randhawa," even though I have spent my entire life as Nikki. It is my middle name and on my birth certificate. I had taken Haley as my last name when Michael and I were married. The message was clear: She's not one of us and she's not from around here. That was the beginning of a barrage of hate mail, angry calls, and intimidation attempts against our family.

I felt defeated and exhausted. One day, Michael and I went to a Thai restaurant. When we received our fortune cookies at the end of our meal, I looked at him and said, "I really need this to say something good." And there it was. I opened it and couldn't believe it. It said, "Winners do what losers don't want to." I taped it to my computer screen. That's when I realized it's not enough to work hard. We have to work smart. But more importantly, we have to go to places that are uncomfortable. Do things that aren't in our comfort zone. Only then do we learn to overcome.

I started going to areas of the district that I assumed I couldn't win. I worked on winning the support of my opponent's family members. I didn't allow them to define me. I put myself out in front of everyone and defined myself for all of them to see.

On Election Night, the returns showed that the great people of Lexington County were better than the slimy tactics and malicious attacks. I went on to win the election 55–45 percent. I went on to win my next election by the largest margin in the state and another one after that. I never lost a race.

The lesson I take away is when you keep fighting, you find out you are so much stronger on the other side.

Golda Meir personified this lesson. Her hurdles were far more formidable than anything I faced, and they pushed her to historic achievements. From Russia to America to the independent Jewish state of Israel, Golda's journey wasn't one that happened to her. It was one she made happen.

Golda Meir

Take Action

Nothing in life just happens. It isn't enough to believe in something; you have to have the stamina to meet obstacles and overcome them, to struggle.[1]

—GOLDA MEIR

Winners do what losers don't want to.

—NIKKI HALEY
(AND A FORTUNE COOKIE)

Golda Meir was one of the most accomplished women of the twentieth century. A founding member of the Jewish state, a member of the Knesset, a labor minister, a foreign minister, Israel's fourth prime minister, the modern world's first female head of state (who did not inherit the position), and a global icon who was identified simply by her first name: Golda. She broke barriers and smashed glass ceilings to smithereens. She defied the odds and overturned society's expectations.

How did she do it? If you asked her, there was no alternative. Doing was the only option.

Her path in life wasn't obvious or easy. Born

to a poor Jewish family in Kyiv, in the Russian empire in 1898, survival was the first hurdle. This was no simple feat, considering five of her older siblings died in infancy. Only three of the Mabovitch children survived—Golda and her two sisters.[2]

Golda had few happy memories of her first eight years. The clearest were hard ones: "poverty, cold, hunger, and fear." Her first memory of a pogrom—a Russian word that refers to a massacre of a particular ethnic group (usually Jews)—was at three and a half years old. She barely knew what it meant. But she knew it was bad, and she knew it happened because she was Jewish.[3]

At age five, the family moved to Pinsk, where the hardship continued. Her father couldn't keep a job and left soon after for America. There was never enough food to go around, and violence was a constant threat. In her autobiography, Golda recalls the sounds. The sound of nails hitting wood as her father boarded up their meager apartment. The sound of hooves clomping from the Russian military's horses. The sound of screams from the police station around the corner.[4]

She was first introduced to Zionism as a young girl in Pinsk, eavesdropping on her sister Sheyna and her friends' weighty conversations. Although the nuances were hard to grasp, she understood the basic idea that Jews needed a place of their own to be safe. A place free from pogroms, from galloping hooves, from the screams at the police station.[5]

The brainchild of Austrian Jew Theodor Herzl, Zionism is a political movement born at the end of the nineteenth century. Herzl believed the Jews needed a homeland of their own to be safe from the constant threat of anti-Semitism, and the best place for that homeland was the historical and biblical home of the Jewish people: Zion, or Jerusalem. Initially, Zionism was rejected and derided across the spectrum of world Jewry for a host of religious, moral, practical, and philosophical reasons.

But not by Golda. Born two years after Herzl wrote *Der Judenstaat* (*The Jewish State*), Golda believed. For her, Zionism was more than a pipe dream. It was an answer. Golda describes the most important lesson she could learn as a poor, Jewish child: "Nothing in life just happens. It isn't enough to believe in something; you have to have the stamina to meet obstacles and overcome them, to struggle."[6]

Life in Russia taught her that no one would save the Jews if they didn't save themselves. This lesson replayed itself throughout her life. During World War I and later during World War II, she saw what happened to her Jewish brothers and sisters when they depended on others, when six million of them were murdered in the Holocaust. If you didn't fight, if you didn't push, there would be no food, no safety, no life, no future. Waiting for something better to come along was not an option.

In 1906, Golda, her two sisters, and her mother made the difficult trip to America to reunite with her father. It was a weeks-long journey that started with sneaking across the Russian border under false names, bribing the police, and hopping from city to city. From Pinsk to Galicia to Vienna to Antwerp to Quebec to Milwaukee—finally, the Mabovitches were reunited in the New World. As hard as that trip was, it saved their lives.[7] Decades later, the rest of Golda's extended family were murdered in the Holocaust.[8]

The lesson was clear: Staying still was a death sentence—sometimes literally. Moving, planning, doing was the only way.

Golda was a problem solver. She was quick on her feet, comfortable on a public stage, and persuasive. In the fourth grade in Milwaukee, she wanted to help her fellow students who couldn't afford the small textbook fee at the local public school. Foreshadowing her future as a fundraiser for the Jewish community in Palestine, she invited the entire school district to a town hall meeting hosted by the American Young Sisters Society—an organization that existed only in Golda's head. At eleven years old, she convinced a hall to rent out a room to her. She ended up raising a sizable sum of money, and her efforts were written up in the local Milwaukee newspaper.[9]

Golda graduated elementary school and had big plans for herself. She wanted an education, and she aspired to accomplish big things. Her parents had other ideas in mind—actually one idea, specifically: marriage. "It doesn't pay to be too clever," her father reprimanded her. "Men don't like smart girls."[10]

But the cake was already baked for Golda. She was smart *and* clever. Most of all, she was stubborn. Her parents' vision for her life was unacceptable to her. She argued, she begged, she cried—to no avail. When at age sixteen Golda discovered her mother was already negotiating her future away to thirtysomething Mr. Goodstein, she made a life-altering decision. She ran away to Denver to stay with her sister Sheyna and her husband.[11]

If renting a hall at age eleven was impressive, traveling secretly across the country at age fifteen was further proof of Golda's stubborn independence. Most girls her age would have given in to their parents' wishes. Few—if any— would have packed their bags, left a note ("I am going to live with Sheyna so that I can study"), kissed their younger sister goodbye, and boarded a train for Denver.[12]

Denver was a different world; it opened Golda's

mind to new possibilities. Not only did she continue her education for the two years she was there but she soaked up every conversation from the rotating cast of intellectuals who frequented Sheyna's home. Politics, Zionism, literature, art, music—Golda consumed every morsel. The discussions of the Jewish homeland interested her most.[13]

It wasn't all doe-eyed idealism. When Golda moved back to Milwaukee, she had the opportunity to meet many of the early Zionist leaders, such as Shmaryahu Levin, Yitzhak Ben-Zvi, and Rachel Yanait, as they passed through the Jewish community. They spoke about the reality on the ground in Palestine, the communities they were building, and the harsh life under the Turks. At this point in her life, Golda didn't know what her future held, but she knew one thing: She wasn't going to be a parlor Zionist—the kind that sat around parlor rooms and *talked* about a Jewish state. She desperately wanted—needed—to be a part of what was to come.[14]

World events interceded to shape Golda's future. Although she had originally planned on being a teacher, there were simply too many other things to do and too many problems to solve. Life for Europe's Jews during World War I was brutal. She joined a Jewish relief group and later got involved in the newly formed American Jewish Congress—an organization created to advocate for Jews in America and all over the world.[15]

Golda's life from 1915 to 1921 was a flurry of activity: She officially joined the Labor Zionist Party and involved herself in all its goings-on; she organized a protest against European pogroms; she took to the road to raise funds for Zionist endeavors; and she served as a delegate to the first American Jewish Congress convention. And, in 1917, she married Morris Meyerson, whom she had met while living in Denver. All these adventures were but preparation for the ultimate adventure: the move to Palestine.[16]

On May 23, 1921, Golda boarded the SS *Pocahontas* with her husband, Morris, her sister, Sheyna, and a group of her closest friends for a long journey that would eventually take them to Palestine. Nothing could prepare them for the disaster that followed. It started with a worker strike that sent the ship back to New York City. A week later, they embarked again. From New York to Boston, to the Azores, to Naples, to Alexandria, to El Qantara, to Tel Aviv, they endured more worker strikes, boat repairs, power cuts, and barely edible food. It was enough for some of her companions to change their minds and return to America. When they finally reached Tel Aviv, one of her friends remarked, "Well, Goldie, you wanted to come to *Eretz Yisroel* [the land of Israel]. Here we are. Now we can all go back—it's enough."[17]

For Golda, it was hardly enough—it was just the beginning. She and Morris moved to Kibbutz Merhavia in northern Israel. Kibbutzim were communal farming settlements worked and managed by the residents and their families. It was backbreaking work, but it was the next stop in Golda's dream.[18]

Despite the poverty, the disease, the calloused skin, and the gnats, Golda loved it. It was a place for her problem-solving skills to shine and for her to fulfill her dream of working the land with her bare hands. She only agreed to leave because Morris was chronically ill, and he refused to raise children in the swamps of the kibbutz.[19]

Golda was happiest when she was busy, but there was a cost to pay for her accomplishments. After taking off some time to have children, she was offered a full-time job in 1928 to serve as the secretary of the Moetzet Hapoalot (Women's Labor Council)—part of the Histadrut, Israel's national trade union. The job required relocating to Tel Aviv and considerable travel in Israel and abroad. She jumped at the opportunity. She left Morris in Jerusalem and brought her son and daughter with her to Tel Aviv.[20]

Throughout her life, she struggled with the weight of mother's guilt. It didn't help that her older sister and mother berated her for turning into a "public person, not a homebody," or that her daughter, Sarah, suffered from medical issues in her youth.[21] As her responsibility grew with the Women's Labor Council, so did her time away. When she traveled abroad—to Brussels, Berlin, England, Zurich, America—she was gone for weeks at a time.[22]

When she was home, she was an attentive mother, cooking, cleaning, fixing her children's clothes, and taking them to doctors' appointments. But she wasn't always home. There were long days and meetings that ran late.[23] There were weeks-long trips that turned into months. She couldn't help wondering if it was enough. Did she do enough? Was she present enough?

A part of her always wondered if the answer was no. In 1930, she wrote an article for a collection of personal stories called *The Plough Woman*. She detailed her complicated and sometimes conflicting feelings as a mother, a Zionist, and a person who was born to make a difference:

> Taken as a whole, the inner struggles and despairs of a mother who goes to work have few parallels. But within that whole, there are many shades and variations. . . . There is a type of woman who cannot remain home for other reasons. In spite of the place which her children and her family take up in her life, her nature and being demand something more; she

cannot divorce herself from a larger social life. She cannot let her children narrow her horizon. And for such a woman, there is no rest.[24]

The work she was doing was important. The Histadrut was more than a labor union. It was the beating heart and soul of the Labor Zionist movement. From the moment she took the job, her life changed dramatically. She later acknowledged that this job—this sacrifice—"put me on the path which led me to sitting in the Prime Minister's office."[25]

Golda quickly became one of the best representatives for the Zionist cause abroad and a prolific fundraiser. It helped that she was young and spoke English fluently. When she traveled, Jews flocked to hear her speak about life on the *Yishuv*—the name for the Jewish community in Palestine that would later become the modern state of Israel. In late 1928, she was sent to America for nine months—the longest time away from her children. She traveled from city to city, on buses and trains, sleeping at friendly homes, even sharing a bed when necessary. With each city, her reputation and celebrity status grew. She regaled American Zionists with stories from the Yishuv and urged them to donate. If they didn't have money, she told them to "do housework for one another or make *lokshen* [noodles] and sell it."[26]

During the 1930s, Golda climbed the ranks of the Histadrut. She became a member of the executive committee, responsible for some of the biggest policy decisions in the Yishuv. And there were big decisions to be made. The situation in Palestine and the world was deteriorating. Arab violence and riots increased throughout the 1930s. There was also a growing division among Zionist leaders—between David Ben-Gurion's Labor Party and Ze'ev Jabotinsky's more nationalist and more aggressive Revisionist Party. At the same time, Hitler's rise to power in Germany brought tens of thousands of immigrants to the Yishuv, all of whom had to be absorbed.[27]

Hitler's rise solidified for Golda what she had long known in her gut: The Jews could depend on no one. In March 1938, Golda attended President Franklin Roosevelt's International Conference on Refugees—eleven days after Germany occupied Austria. She listened to a broken record of nations explaining why they couldn't accept Jewish refugees and said, "There is only one thing I hope to see before I die, and that is that my people should not need expressions of sympathy anymore."[28]

She threw herself into action the only way she knew how. She organized protests and strikes against the British White Paper—a 1939 document issued by British prime minister

Neville Chamberlain severely limiting Jewish immigration to Palestine. She was directly involved in a furtive effort to smuggle European Jews into Palestine. Between 1937 and 1939, tens of thousands of immigrants arrived in Palestine thanks to these efforts.[29]

Golda was undeterred. She argued passionately for the immigration efforts to continue at all costs. She did not know at the time—few did—how much these efforts mattered. Several years later, when news of Nazi concentration camps and gas chambers trickled out, Golda and her fellow Zionists could hardly believe it. "It wasn't that we were gullible," she said. "It was simply that we couldn't conceive of what was then still inconceivable."[30]

The shock gave way to a need to act. Everything changed in the final years of the war. While her fellow Zionists debated how much time and resources they should devote to rescuing Europe's Jews, there was no debate for Golda. "There is no other Zionism now except for the rescue of Jews," she declared. Traditional Zionism—building up the land and establishing cities and towns—took a back seat. She took it upon herself to raise as much money as possible to aid the rescue efforts. She was often rebuffed. Many Jews thought there was little they could do, and the money would never achieve its intended purpose. But Golda was dogged, even desperate.

With each rejection, she got creative. She gathered one hundred Jews in a room and told them they couldn't leave until each one wrote a check for a thousand pounds. It worked.[31]

She pursued every avenue she could think of. She begged Jewish American and British leaders to intercede with their respective country's political class, but Golda was unimpressed with their reactions.[32] After Germany invaded Hungary and began deporting Hungarian Jews by the thousands to the Auschwitz death camp, she implored Allied leaders to bomb the railroad lines to stop the deportations. She begged the British chief secretary for a ship to save as many Jewish children as possible. "Don't you know there's a war on?" he asked incredulously. "I have heard there is war," Golda replied. "But if they were British children, would you find a ship for them?"[33] Each time, the answer was no.

These years were brutal. Golda threw herself into her work, taking each loss personally. She was deeply disappointed in her fellow Jews. Whether they could have done more is up for debate, but Golda fiercely believed that they should have tried. They "should have turned the world upside down," she said.[34] After all, that is what she did.

It was reminiscent of her early days in Kyiv, watching her father board up the windows of their meager home, wishing desperately there was something more that could be done.[35] She despised what she called "the curse of helplessness."[36] Taking action was the only antidote.

Even after the war ended, the work didn't stop. With hundreds of thousands of Jewish survivors sitting in camps all across Europe, the Zionists were desperate to bring them to Palestine. They had an ally in President Harry Truman, who urged the British government to relax its immigration quotas for Palestine. British foreign secretary Ernest Bevin rejected their pleas. Worse, he threatened the Zionists with renewed anti-Semitism even as the ashes of European Jewry still burned. "If the Jews with all their sufferings want to get too much at the head of the queue," he said, "you have the danger of another anti-Semitic reaction through it all."[37]

Golda held nothing back in her response:

> We know what our strength is. Our strength is the strength of a despairing nation that is fighting and struggling now for its life. . . . Many of us face the question of whether to die with honor or to die as cowards. . . . We have received the declaration of war by the English government—we will not answer it by giving in.[38]

Throughout 1946, the moderate Zionists (to which Golda belonged) united with the militant factions against the British.[39] They blew up buildings and bridges and continued to smuggle Jewish refugees into Palestine. When the British refused to allow a ship filled with Jewish refugees into Palestine, the ship's passengers adopted a hunger strike. Golda, then recovering from a near heart attack, convinced her fellow leaders to join the hunger strike in solidarity. Sixteen days after the British intercepted the ship, the hunger strike ended; the British had relented. After fasting for 101 hours, Golda and her colleagues celebrated.[40]

As both sides ratcheted up attacks, the British retaliated by arresting as many Zionist leaders as they could and exiling those who were abroad. For whatever reason, Golda was not included—a badge of dishonor in her mind. But in the summer and fall of 1946, with so many of her fellow leaders sidelined, her leadership position grew. She played an instrumental role in rejecting the Morrison-Grady Plan—a partition plan that would continue to give the British control over the Jewish area and deny the Zionists the one thing they wanted: a Jewish state.[41]

Fed up with the ongoing turmoil, the British turned over the Palestine problem to the newly formed United Nations. On November 29, 1947, thirty-three countries voted yes on a partition plan that gave the Jews their state. The Jews celebrated, but the Zionists' leaders knew what lay ahead. The Arabs rejected the UN resolution, and war was coming.[42]

They were right. As Arab attacks increased into 1948, the Jews of Palestine were in an increasingly precarious position. Jerusalem was under siege, cut off from supplies and food, and British soldiers still stationed in Palestine did little to protect Jewish areas from violence. The Jews needed arms. But to get arms, they needed money. Golda stepped up again, volunteering to go back to America and raise the funds for the Zionists' arms-smuggling campaign.[43]

This might have been her most important mission yet. She needed to raise millions of dollars and fast. She didn't have the luxury of waiting three or four months. As she crisscrossed the United States, David Ben-Gurion purchased guns, airplanes, and other equipment on faith that Golda would be successful. His faith was well placed. She raised $25 million. When she returned to Israel in March 1948, Ben-Gurion welcomed her with high praise: "Someday when history will be written, it will be said that there was a Jewish woman who got the money which made the state possible."[44]

It was not an exaggeration. In April, the Zionists launched Operation Nachshon—a military campaign to save Jerusalem and go on the offensive. Thousands of rifles, machine guns, and bullets were smuggled out of Czechoslovakia with the money Golda raised. Not only did they liberate Jerusalem, the Jewish army—the Haganah—took control of many of the cities granted to the Jews under the UN partition plan, including the port city of Haifa.[45]

This would all become more important as the British prepared to leave and the neighboring Arab countries—Syria, Lebanon, Transjordan, Egypt, and Iraq—prepared to attack. At midnight on May 14, 1948, the British left Palestine for good. The British Mandate was over. At 4:00 a.m., Ben-Gurion read Israel's Declaration of Independence: "We hereby declare the establishment of a Jewish state in *Eretz* Israel, to be known as *Medinat Yisrael*, the State of Israel." Golda Meir—then Meyerson—signed her name with tears running down her face, thinking of all that had happened to make this historic moment possible. She thought about all the people they had lost, all the sacrifices they had made, all the hoping, dreaming, and fighting when no one thought it was possible. It was the greatest, most important day of her life.[46]

After the Holocaust, the words *never again* became a rallying cry, often used to signal the world's resolve against a similar atrocity. Never again will we allow hatred and evil to grow and thrive. Never again will we allow one group of people to decimate another. But Golda had a different version of *never again*. Never again will Jews be dependent on others for their security and safety. Never again will the Jewish people be defenseless before their enemies. Never again will they be victims.

Golda is well known for her stubbornness, but it wasn't just stubbornness that pushed her to the height of Israeli leadership. It was her resourcefulness. While others threw up their hands and asked, "What can we do?" Golda asked a different question: "What happens if we do nothing?" Doing was the only option.

The story of Golda Meir—much like the story of Zionism—is a lesson in sheer will. For centuries, Jews had been chased and beaten, oppressed and murdered. From the Crusades to the Inquisition, from the pogroms to the Holocaust, restraint and inaction ended in tragedy. What did she do? Golda joined a ramshackle group of Jews in a desolate land, filled with desert and few natural resources. They begged, borrowed, and built. When they needed water, they figured out how to extract it from the desert. When they were under attack, they built an army. When they needed arms, they found a way to smuggle them. When they needed money to buy arms, they raised millions of dollars. When their fellow Jews needed help, they snuck as many of them into Palestine as possible.

There is great power in the desperate will to survive. Golda understood that. It had been goading her to action her whole life. That will pushed her to succeed because there was no other choice. In the Yishuv, there was a saying, succinct and powerful in its Hebrew: *"Ein breira"*—"There is no alternative."[47]

She could have stayed in Russia and perished. She could have stayed in the comfort of America. She could have stayed home more, traveled less, pushed less. She could have given up hope in the darkest hour. She could have stopped working when she collapsed and was hospitalized with a near heart attack. She could have rested more and given up chain-smoking—which fueled her existence as much as the blood in her veins. She could have stopped when she collapsed *again.* Perhaps a different person could have, but she could not. *Ein breira.* There is no alternative. The only option was to fight, she said, "not in the ghettos, not in gas chambers, but here in the Land of Israel."[48]

It would be another twenty-one years before she became Israel's prime minister in 1969. By that time, Golda Meir had already cemented her place in the history of her people and the world.

Zionism was just an idea, some might say a dream. If not for the men and women who put in the sweat and tears to make the Jewish state a reality, it would have stayed an idea. The world is filled with big ideas, but most of them stay just that—ideas. In politics, you meet a lot of big talkers, people who promise you the world but have no intention of lifting a finger if they get elected. We need more doers—people willing to take on the tough fights and put in the long nights. It's easy to mistake noise for action, but those are not the same thing. Often, it is the quiet, determined people who put in the work while someone else gets the credit.

Life is no different. We all know people who talk a good game but don't deliver. Let's not sugarcoat it: Taking action is hard and scary. Some people are lazy. Some people are terrified of failure. Some people don't know where to begin. The answer is: You start with the first step. You start with a leap of faith, knowing that falling is just a part of the process.

The world we live in doesn't always reward action. Smart takes on Twitter and cute Instagram videos can make you famous without doing anything meaningful. Remember, social media isn't real life. Those viral moments are fleeting. Those "friends" might disappear as quickly as they appeared. The people who change the world are the ones who don't care about going viral. They don't measure their success by followers or media hits. They measure success by the goals achieved, by the lives changed, by the dreams realized.

Golda's story is a story of building something from nothing. It was that much harder because much of the world was rooting for the Jews to fail, and some were actively trying to destroy them. Golda and her colleagues knew that it's much harder to dismantle than deny. So, the Zionists didn't give the world a chance to deny them. They built roads, schools, and hospitals with their bare hands. They established towns and cities. They created an army and smuggled weapons to outfit their soldiers. By the time 1948 came around, the Jews had built a state even before the United Nations gave its official blessing.

It doesn't matter what you did or didn't do yesterday. It only matters what you decide to do today. Will you take the first step? Will you take a second? Will you make that leap of faith across the unknown?

We all have the power to change the world in our own way. But nothing will happen and nothing will change if we don't take decisive action. Is it easy? Nothing worth having ever comes easily. Is it guaranteed? There are no guarantees. But is it worth it? Yes. No matter what happens, the work you put in will shape you and shape those around you. You will change lives—starting with your own.

4

Some of the stories in this book are uplifting. They bring a smile to our faces and put a little extra oomph in our step. This is a different kind of story. It is painful and raw, and it doesn't have a happy ending. But that's why it's so important to tell. Because sometimes life is filled with dark, soul-crushing moments. It's how we use those moments for good that makes the difference.

I met Cindy Warmbier in 2017 under the worst possible circumstances. Her twenty-two-year-old son, Otto, had been imprisoned in North Korea for more than a year, stuck in one of the most evil and most barbaric countries in the world.

It is hard to overstate how terrible life is in Kim Jong-un's hell on Earth. For seventy-five years, North Koreans have lived under the Kim dynasty with no rights. No freedom of religion. No freedom of expression. No independent media. No right to due process. No property rights. No freedom of movement. Nearly all aspects of their daily lives are controlled by the Communist government. Those who dare to defy the regime are imprisoned, sent to forced labor camps, made to disappear, or killed.

For twelve months, Cindy watched and waited as the Obama administration told her to be patient. They told her not to speak and they would handle it. But her son was being held captive by a madman. He was a political pawn in Kim Jong-un's heinous propaganda machine. She was done being patient.

I am a mom, and her story ripped my heart in two. As a former governor who saw lives destroyed by hate crimes and natural disasters, I had experienced my share of pain and sadness. As the UN ambassador who saw evil up close all over the world, I was furious. I wanted so badly to help.

Cindy embodied strength. She didn't hide her emotions; she channeled them into her actions. At first, her mission was to bring her son home. After Otto's death, she focused (and continues to focus) her attention on making North Korea pay.

I drew inspiration from Cindy's courage and a belief that Kim needed to pay for what he did to Otto and his constant threats to the world. I, too, had no patience for the Obama administration's policy of "strategic patience"—as it was called.

On August 5, 2017, just two months after Otto's death, the United Nations unanimously passed worldwide sanctions on North Korea—the largest set of sanctions against North Korea and the largest set of sanctions against any country in a generation.

Every time I went to battle against North Korea, I thought about Otto. Cindy and Fred Warmbier gave me a necklace with a pendant that spelled Otto's name, and I made sure to wear it whenever I spoke about North Korea.

During my time at the United Nations, I made it my mission to reach out to dissidents and families of hostages from dictatorial countries and highlight their stories on the global stage. I did this for two reasons. I wanted to show these brave men and women that we had their backs. We would be their voice, and they were not alone. The other reason was to put the world's worst human rights abusers on notice. Yes, the United Nations has a terrible record on human rights. It routinely looks the other way when dictators commit horrific crimes. But we can never be one of those nations who looks away. We should always speak for those who can't speak for themselves.

We will never forget Otto and the many other American lives we have lost to evil tyrants. I promised Cindy I would keep fighting to show the world the evil that exists. I promised myself I would never forget Otto and the strength of women like Cindy, who face unspeakable horrors with steel and guts. Cindy is an inspiration to women everywhere; we don't stop and we never give up.

Cindy Warmbier

Be Strong

They're not going to win. I'm never, ever giving up this fight. I'm very patient. I'm not going away.[1]

—CINDY WARMBIER

I will not shut up. Rather, I will respectfully speak some hard truths.[2]

—NIKKI HALEY

Nothing can prepare a mother for her worst nightmare. And when that nightmare descends, it feels like being crushed by the weight of the world. Everything else stops. Nothing else matters. Except for getting her son back alive and healthy.

For Cindy and Fred Warmbier, that nightmare began January 2, 2016. Every day after is forever tainted by the darkness that consumed their lives. Every day before is a memory of a better time.

Cindy and Fred were suburban Cincinnati parents, raising their three children and living the American dream. Fred started and built up a successful metal-finishing business.[3] Cindy worked part-time at the business and raised their children.[4] Their oldest, Otto, was a smart, talented, and fun-loving boy. He played soccer and swam, got top grades at his Ohio high school, and was a math whiz. He was homecoming king, salutatorian, and Student of the Year. He was everyone's friend.[5] After high school, he went to the University of Virginia (UVA), where he majored in economics.[6]

After securing a finance internship the fall of his junior year, he decided to take a trip abroad over UVA's January term. Curious about other cultures, he enrolled in a study-abroad program in Hong Kong and Singapore. Traveling to far-flung countries was natural for him. At age twenty-one, he had already been to Cuba, Israel, and the Galapagos Islands. Since he was already flying halfway around the world, he decided to visit North Korea.[7]

While North Korea is a repressive society that doesn't allow its people to come and go as they please, it allows thousands of foreigners to visit as part of very controlled tourist groups. One such group is a Chinese company called Young Pioneer Tours, which offers tours to "destinations your mother would rather you stay away from." Otto submitted a $1,200 deposit for a five-day, four-night tour.[8]

After Christmas in 2015, Otto met the rest of his tour group at the Beijing airport, where they boarded a flight for Pyongyang. When they arrived in North Korea, border police took their cameras and searched their phones. They had stepped into a different world, a world in which freedom did not exist.[9]

The tour was an odd mix of North Korean propaganda and vacation fun. They visited the American navy ship USS *Pueblo* and were treated to the story about how North Korea captured the ship in 1968 from the "imperial enemy." This became a running joke among the group—a mix of Americans, Canadians, Europeans, and Australians—who referred to Otto as the "imperial enemy."[10]

On New Year's Eve, the group celebrated the new year with locals in Pyongyang's main square. Afterward, they returned to the hotel, which offered an array of entertainment, including five restaurants, a sauna, a bar, and a bowling alley. Otto's British roommate, Danny Gratton, went bowling and didn't keep tabs on his American friend. When Gratton returned to their room at 4:30 a.m. on the first day of 2016, Otto was sound asleep.[11]

The next morning, Danny and Otto were the final members of the group to show their passports at the airport. Danny remembers the officers studying the passports for an unusually long time. Then two soldiers tapped Otto on the shoulder and took him away. Danny joked, "Well, that's the last we'll ever see of you."[12]

Turns out, it wasn't a joke. That was the beginning of the nightmare.

Cindy and Fred texted Otto on New Year's Day—January 2 in China—expecting him to say he had landed safely in Beijing. They heard nothing. They followed up with the tour group only to be told that Otto had missed his flight and would be on the next flight out. He wasn't.[13]

In Washington, D.C., State Department official Robert King returned to work after the long weekend and reached out to the Warmbiers. King was the special envoy for North Korean human-rights issues and had helped Americans come home from North Korea's prison system.[14] King urged the Warmbiers to keep a low profile and allow the State Department to do its job through back channels. A public campaign might aggravate Korean dictator Kim Jong-un, and he might take it out on Otto. Most importantly, he assured them that Otto would be released soon.[15]

The next few months played out like scenes from a horror movie. In late February 2016, Otto confessed on video to "the crime of taking down a political slogan" from a wall in the hotel he was staying in. The Warmbiers watched a ghostly Otto declare, "I apologize to each and every one of the millions of the Korean people. . . . I wish that the United States administration never manipulate people like myself in the future to commit crimes against foreign countries."[16]

According to his testimony, Otto took the poster at the behest of the Friendship United Methodist Church, which offered him a used car in exchange for bringing the poster back as a "trophy."[17] The confession was filled with absurd details that could not be corroborated and made no sense to anyone who knew Otto. For example, Otto was Jewish and had no ties to the Methodist church.[18] It was part of North Korea's typical playbook—force the American to give a coerced confession, play the videotape publicly to highlight America's hostility, use the American as a bargaining chip in a game of three-dimensional geopolitical chess.

This was the first time Otto's parents had seen him since he left home. It would be the last time they would hear his voice. Two weeks later, Otto was sentenced to fifteen years of prison and hard labor after a one-hour sham trial.[19]

The Warmbiers grew frustrated with the State Department's lack of progress.[20] They turned elsewhere. Bill Richardson, the former governor of New Mexico and UN ambassador under Bill Clinton, headed a foundation that engaged in "fringe diplomacy" to help free Americans trapped in authoritarian countries. From February to August 2016, Richardson or his colleague traveled to New York periodically to meet with

North Korea's representative at the United Nations. After several months, it was clear: Conversations were not enough.[21]

Richardson secured permission to send his senior advisor, Mickey Bergman, to North Korea to try to get some answers. In September 2016, Bergman met with North Korean officials "in the first face-to-face meeting between American and North Korean representatives in Pyongyang in nearly two years." Bergman wasn't allowed to see Otto.[22]

Cindy and Fred were already terrified and desperate. With each passing day, they grew angrier. A year had passed since they lost their son to the dungeons of North Korea, and they didn't know if he was dead or alive. America was the most powerful country in the world, and the State Department couldn't even confirm that basic information. When they met with Secretary of State John Kerry, Cindy begged him to save her son. His response? North Korea will let us know what it wants.[23]

Cindy didn't know what to do. Her instincts cried out to fight for her son, but the Obama administration insisted that following her gut would only *hurt* Otto more.

Her instincts won out. The State Department had failed and lied to them one too many times. Besides, a new administration now occupied the White House, and the Trump administration was nothing like its predecessor. Early in 2017, Cindy and Fred appeared on Fox News, hoping to catch the new president's attention. They held nothing back. They criticized the State Department for not doing enough and begged, "President Trump, I ask you: Bring my son home. You can make a difference here."[24]

Their efforts paid off. In June 2017, seventeen months after Otto disappeared, the Trump administration informed North Korea that an American plane would be landing in Pyongyang with the express purpose of bringing Otto home. Ohio senator Rob Portman called the Warmbiers with good news. Otto was on a plane, and it had just entered Japanese airspace. But it wasn't all good news. Otto had been unconscious for more than a year.[25]

Cindy and Fred didn't know what to expect. They braced for the worst and hoped for the best. But nothing could prepare them for the moment they laid eyes on their son. They heard a deep growling sound—they described it as inhuman. Otto was strapped to a stretcher, his deformed limbs jerking. His hair was gone, his teeth misshapen, and a feeding tube was placed in his nostrils. The friendly, smart boy they had raised was unresponsive. His body was there, but he was a shell of who he used to be.[26] Cindy later remarked that it looked "like he'd seen the devil, and he had."[27]

On June 19, 2017, six days after coming home, Otto died.[28] He was twenty-two years old.

That could have been the end of the story. But the Warmbiers believed it was just the beginning. Cindy and Fred dedicated their lives to finding justice for their son and telling the world the truth about the evil that exists in North Korea.

After Otto's death, the North Korean government denied any mistreatment, claiming Otto's vegetative state was the result of botulism poisoning.[29] The regime hailed itself the "biggest victim" of a "smear campaign" orchestrated by the United States. It went on to say, "Although we had no reason at all to show mercy to such a criminal of the enemy state, we provided him with medical treatments and care with all sincerity on humanitarian basis until his return to the U.S."[30]

Three months later, Cindy and Fred spoke out. They shared with the world the painful, gruesome details of Otto's homecoming. They relived the cruel moment when they realized their son was never coming back to them. They told the world how evil regimes operate.[31] "North Korea is not a victim. They're terrorists," Fred told Fox News. "They kidnapped Otto. They tortured him. They intentionally injured him. They are not victims."[32]

Cindy and Fred made it their mission to target North Korea in any way they could.

In 2018, Cindy spoke at a UN symposium on human rights, explaining, "I can't let Otto die in vain. . . . We're not special, but we're Americans and we know what freedom's like, and we have to stand up for this. We have to."[33] They also spoke out against diplomatic efforts with Kim Jong-un. "North Korea to me is a cancer on the Earth," Cindy declared at a 2019 press conference. "How can you have diplomacy with someone who never tells the truth? We're dealing with absolute evil."[34]

The Warmbiers' vigilance produced concrete results. In November 2017, President Trump redesignated North Korea as a state sponsor of terror, nearly ten years after it had been removed.[35] In 2019, Congress passed and President Trump signed the bipartisan Otto Warmbier Banking Restrictions Involving North Korea (BRINK) Act. The bill imposed mandatory sanctions on foreign banks and companies that do business with North Korea. Cindy and Fred came to Washington to mark the occasion just a few days after Otto's twenty-fifth birthday. "People matter. Otto matters," Cindy said. "We're never going to let you forget our son."[36]

They also went after North Korea's money directly. President Trump's designation of North Korea as a state sponsor of terror opened a legal path for the Warmbiers to sue the regime for brutally torturing and murdering their son.[37] In the final days of 2018, a federal judge ordered North Korea to pay the Warmbiers $501 million, arguing the heavy damages were necessary to punish North Korea and prevent the regime from imprisoning, torturing, and killing others.[38]

The decision was a victory for Otto and sent an important message to Kim Jong-un and other evil dictators around the world. But extracting the $501 million would not be easy. So, Cindy and Fred began tracking North Korea's extensive money trail. They targeted North Korean embassies across Eastern Europe that operated illegal businesses in violation of international sanctions. They succeeded in shutting down a hostel business run out of North Korea's Berlin embassy.[39] In America, they went after the millions of dollars of North Korea's frozen assets sitting in U.S. banks.[40] Perhaps most importantly, Cindy and Fred's efforts inspired similar legal action in Japan[41] and South Korea.[42]

North Korea was responsible for Cindy and Fred's worst nightmare. Now, the Warmbiers are returning the favor. North Korea will never be free of them. Everywhere the regime turns, Cindy and Fred Warmbier will be there, fighting, denouncing, and making it pay—literally.

A mother's love is a powerful force—maybe the most powerful. It pushed Cindy to fight for Otto when the Obama administration told the Warmbiers to be quiet and trust the system. And it pushed her to keep on fighting after Otto died. "I just want to tell North Korea, as long as I'm alive, no one's going to forget what you did to Otto," she told *60 Minutes Australia*. "I'm not going to let them. I'm not going away. I'm in it for the long haul. I'm just patiently waiting because the day is going to come when that regime is over."[43]

To this day, Cindy's love for Otto is her motivation. She continues to live her life because that is what Otto would have wanted. She continues to be a mother to her two other children. She seeks justice for Otto's memory, and she fights to make sure there are no other American lives lost to North Korea's torture machine.[44]

Cindy told me one of her proudest moments came in a Los Angeles courtroom in the spring of 2021.[45] In some ways, it felt like she was reliving her nightmare over again. She was crying, pleading with the U.S. government to spare a young man's life from North Korea's clutches. But this young man wasn't her Otto. He was a Korean American named Christopher Ahn.

Ahn was a U.S. Marine who served in Iraq. After leaving the military, he became involved with a group that helped North Korean defectors. In 2019, he joined the group on a mission to Madrid to help a North Korean diplomat defect from the regime's embassy there. The diplomat balked at the last minute, and the group abandoned the mission. Ahn returned home to his family in California and went on with his life. Two months later, U.S. Marshals arrested Ahn, charging him with being party to an illegal raid on North Korea's Spanish embassy (Ahn asserts that they were invited into the building). He spent three months in a federal prison and is fighting extradition to Spain, where he is certain North Korea will have him killed. The FBI had already informed Ahn of North Korean threats on his life. In Spain, North Korea could easily use its diplomatic presence on the ground to make an enemy like Christopher disappear.[46]

Cindy didn't know Christopher Ahn. Their only connection was that she knew what North Korea would do to Christopher. And she knew the bureaucrats at the U.S. Department of Justice would not fight for Christopher's life unless someone made them fight. That someone was Cindy.

With tears streaming down her face, she told a federal judge, "No one will stand up to North Korea. I'm left standing up to North Korea— me. . . . I know now they will kill Christopher Ahn. I don't know Christopher Ahn, but in my book . . . he's a hero." She continued,

I begged the State Department. Please bring him home. He didn't do anything.

"Oh, he'll be OK. He'll be OK." That's what they told me. That's what they'll say about Chris. He'll be OK. I'm sorry I'm so emotional. I'm sorry that I'm begging you, but the only thing I can do is stand up to North Korea and pray that more people will stand up to them. Please.[47]

Cindy Warmbier had no aspirations of being a public-facing leader. She didn't relish the spotlight or enjoy speaking to large groups. When life handed her the worst possible news, she fought through the fear and anguish. She spoke out even while tears rolled down her cheeks. She told the truth about one of the world's most evil regimes, and she didn't back down.

When a parent loses a child, they lose a piece of themselves, and they are forever haunted by the emptiness left behind. That emptiness can be all-consuming. It hurts in a physical way, gnawing at a person's existence. It can make life unbearable.

Cindy Warmbier felt all these things and more. In her worst moment, she summoned the strength she needed to fight for her son, to demand justice for his death, and to stand up to totalitarian thugs on the world stage. If you ask Cindy where that strength came from, she will tell you, "It came from Otto." I will forever look at Cindy as one of the strongest, bravest, and best moms I know.

Courage can mean all kinds of things. Courage

is a soldier diving into the heat of battle. Courage is a child standing up to his tormentors. Courage is embarking on a new and scary challenge. Courage can also mean putting one foot in front of the other, refusing to give up and give in to darkness, and demanding more from the life we are given. Courage is living even when life feels unlivable.

We all face our own demons. Some people are born with them. For others, the demons descend with no warning. As a governor and UN ambassador, I have hugged people in their darkest moments. I have met with mothers, fathers, daughters, and sons who lost everything. I have seen unbelievable strength in the shadows of tragedy. These men and women are my heroes.

Life can be cruel. But we are given just one life with all the wrinkles, warts, and what-ifs. No matter how painful it gets, know that you are not alone. Other strong, courageous people have pushed through the pain and found strength. You can, too.

5

This is not an easy chapter to read—or write. But it is a necessary one. Nadia's story is one of the most painful, heart-rending, inspiring stories I have heard. It is sadder still because she is not alone. She speaks for thousands of women just like her who have endured more pain and suffering than a human should bear.

In 2014, Nadia was twenty-one years old and living in northern Iraq with her family. She had dreams: finish high school, get married, have a family, raise her children in the tight-knit Yazidi community she grew up in. It was a simple life, a hard life, but a life filled with family, love, and God.

That year, her village was wiped out by ISIS militants. While most Americans knew about ISIS and the war consuming the Middle East, few people had heard of the Yazidis or the genocide that was taking place. In her autobiography, Nadia paints a terrifying picture of what she and her community endured.

Many of her family members, friends, and neighbors were killed. She—and thousands of women like her—were taken captive and sold as sex slaves to militants who treated them like objects. None of this was accidental. It was part of an intentional plan on the part of ISIS to destroy the Yazidi people.

Nadia's book details her daring escape and her search for justice. She promised herself she would deny the ISIS terrorists the thing they wanted: her submission. She would not be silent. She would tell the world what she experienced and make it act.

In March 2017, I met with Nadia and her lawyer to help them fight for a resolution at the UN Security Council that would launch an investigative unit to gather evidence that could eventually be used to put ISIS militants in prison for war crimes.[1] The council unanimously approved the resolution, and today the investigation has saved countless pieces of evidence that will make sure the Yazidi people can get the justice they deserve.[2]

In the short time I spent with Nadia, I was moved by her composure, her courage, and her commitment. Navigating the bureaucratic maze at the United Nations can be daunting and discouraging. She never wavered. She never gave up. She knows there are too many women counting on her to succeed.

Her story is one of many. Nadia has the unique ability to make people see, feel, and acknowledge the evil she and so many Yazidis faced. Her story needs to be told and never forgotten.

Nadia Murad

Take Control

I want to be the last girl in the world with a story like mine.[3]

—NADIA MURAD

Your stories are painful. But hearing them helps us stay vigilant. And that vigilance helps ensure that these generations of survivors' stories will, God willing, be the last.[4]

—NIKKI HALEY

Nadia Murad is no stranger to labels. Orphan. Rape victim. Slave. Refugee. These experiences could have easily defined her—if she let them.

She did not.

Nadia wrote a book—*The Last Girl*—about her ordeal as an ISIS sex slave, but that is just a sliver of her story. The inspiring part is what she did afterward. How she fashioned a life for herself on the ashes of tragedy. How she became a human rights leader and a voice for thousands of women like her. Fate dealt her the cruelest of hands. But when given the chance, she made sure that would not be the end of her story. She made sure to write her own.

Nadia Murad's story begins in Kocho, a small Yazidi village of two thousand people in the Sinjar region of northern Iraq.[5] Yazidism is an ancient, monotheistic religion mostly concentrated in Iraq, Syria, and Turkey. Often deemed "nonbelievers" by their Arab neighbors and almost always a minority, Yazidis were persecuted throughout history.[6]

In 2014, Nadia was a twenty-one-year-old wiry farm girl on the verge of finishing high school. She lived in a one-story mud-brick house with her mother, six of her eight brothers, two sisters, two sisters-in-law, and a bevy of young children. The rest of her brothers, half-siblings, aunts, and uncles lived within walking distance.[7]

By any Western standard, life in Kocho was hard. Farming in Iraq was backbreaking work, made unbearable in Iraq's stifling summers. Iraq was also torn apart by war and violence. Survival was a privilege. Too many men, women, and children were lost to treatable illnesses, battle, and violence.[8]

Still, Nadia loved her family and her village. She loved sitting by the hearth talking to her mother as she baked bread in the early hours of the morning. She loved the comfort of the Yazidi traditions and the sense of community. She loved knowing everyone she cared about was close by, and she never felt alone. She loved makeup and dreamed of opening a salon one day so she could help women and girls see themselves as beautiful. Kocho was home. It was the only life she knew, and she couldn't imagine living anywhere else.[9]

All that changed in 2013. An extremist group called the Islamic State of Iraq and al-Sham—ISIS—sprang up in neighboring Syria. It was only a matter of time before ISIS—or *Daesh* in Arabic—crossed into Iraq. By June 2014, ISIS captured Mosul, Iraq's second-largest city, located eighty miles east of Kocho.[10]

The security situation deteriorated fast. Some people fled to the nearby mountain, where they nearly starved to death. But many stayed in Kocho. The Yazidis were proud and loyal. They had built homes, businesses, and lives, and they refused to give them up. Besides, they had nowhere to go.[11]

ISIS arrived on Kocho's doorstep on August 3, 2014. Nadia was sleeping on the roof of her home—the only way to escape the thick summer heat. She woke up to the sound of ISIS trucks rumbling "like grenades in the quiet rural air." One of Nadia's brothers went to get more information and returned home with terrifying news: "Daesh has surrounded Kocho. It is not possible to leave."[12]

They called everyone they knew—in Kurdish Iraq, in Turkey, in America. They begged their

Arab neighbors, teachers, and friends for help. "Someone will come to help us," another brother assured her.[13]

Nobody came. Nobody helped.

For a week and a half, ISIS laid siege to Kocho, while Nadia and her family waited. They didn't eat, bathe, or work the farm. They sat and waited, fantasizing about being rescued. They waited even as the stench became unbearable. The power ran out, and they waited in the dark, only turning on the generator to charge their cell phones and catch a glimpse of the news on TV. There was nothing to do except wait. They waited for a death sentence.[14]

On August 12, the waiting came to an end. An ISIS militant delivered an ultimatum: convert to Islam or suffer the consequences. Two days later, ISIS gathered the entire town in the local school building, separating the men from the women and children. Nadia, her sisters, and her mother were forced inside, where she watched from a second-story window as her brothers, friends, and neighbors were loaded onto trucks and driven away. A minute later, she heard gunshots and screams from behind the school. Her mother, who was the strongest person Nadia knew, collapsed. "They've killed my sons," she cried.[15]

Nadia would later learn that the militants crammed the men into massive ditches like sardines. Then the militants shot them, bullets flying, bodies falling on top of each other. The few who survived managed to play dead under the heavy weight of corpses until they could flee to the mountain.[16]

Back at the school, the militants separated the single women and girls from the mothers and young children. Nadia clung to her mother, refusing to leave, until a militant dragged her away by her armpits and forced her on a bus.[17]

Only then did she learn what the ISIS terrorists had planned for her and her fellow Yazidi women. It started with the man on the bus, a thirty-five-year-old militant named Abu Batat. As the bus rolled along, he walked up and down the aisle, stopping to grope the women. "Every second with ISIS was part of a slow, painful death—of the body and the soul—and that moment on the bus with Abu Batat was the moment I started dying," Nadia wrote.[18]

That's when Nadia earned another label: *sabiyya*, the Arabic word for the sex slaves ISIS captured and exploited like human property. While rape is forbidden in Islam, ISIS claimed Yazidi girls were infidels, and raping an infidel was allowed.[19]

When they arrived in Mosul, the slave market began. ISIS men paced the room while the girls screamed and begged for mercy. The men didn't care. They inspected each girl, tugging at her hair and mouth, demanding to know if she was a virgin.[20]

Nadia was bought by a man named Hajji Salman, who told her, "God wants us to convert you, and if we can't, then we can do what we like to you."[21] The next day, Hajji Salman dragged Nadia to the Mosul courthouse, where she joined a long line of girls who looked just like her, their terrified eyes—the only part of their bodies exposed to the outside world—peeking through their niqabs. She was forced to convert to Islam and fill out paperwork declaring Hajji Salman her rightful owner.[22]

Then, Hajji Salman took her home and raped her. Over and over again. He told her there was no point in trying to escape because she was ruined. No one would want her now, not even her family. It was hard not to believe him. He also warned that there would be terrible consequences if she tried to escape. And it was hard not to believe that, too.[23]

He took her virginity, her body, her religion, and her soul. He beat her, yelled at her, and belittled her. ISIS left nothing but the shell of human flesh. It was a deliberate process to break down the human spirit and wipe out the Yazidi people.

There were times when Nadia wished for the militants to kill her and put her out of her misery.

She already felt dead inside; she might as well be dead on the outside, too. Sometimes, she thought about killing herself. But her mother's words pulled her back to the world of the living. "You have to believe that God will take care of you."[24]

When Nadia was a young girl, she had a terrible accident on the family farm. Day after day, her mother stayed by her hospital bed, willing her back to health. Her mother believed her life was worthwhile. As Nadia endured a living nightmare at the hands of ISIS, each day worse than the one before, she clung to that memory. It kept her alive when she felt depleted. It protected her from the temptation to give up.[25]

When Nadia got a chance to escape, she took it. The militants' biggest mistake was dressing the Yazidi girls like every other Muslim woman living in ISIS-controlled Mosul. In the full-body niqab, it was easy for Nadia to blend in and almost impossible to tell one girl from the next.[26]

But her escape was over before it began. She was captured before she had a chance to leave the property, and her punishment was even more horrific than she could have imagined. Hajji Salman made her undress and reminded her of his promise: "Nadia, I told you that if you tried to escape something really bad would happen to you." Hajji Salman left the room, but six others entered. One by one, the men climbed on top of her and raped her. Then, Hajji Salman sold her.[27]

Her life was an endless series of rapes. Each time, she died again. "At some point, there was rape and nothing else," Nadia wrote. "Your past life becomes a distant memory, like a dream. Your body doesn't belong to you, and there's no energy to talk or to fight or think about the world outside. There is only rape and the numbness that comes with accepting that this is now your life."[28]

After three months in captivity, Nadia got another chance at freedom. The man who bought her left her alone in the house and the door unlocked. She couldn't believe it. She expected a militant to jump out and grab her at any moment, but this time, no one came. She walked and walked until the day turned to night. She knew she couldn't escape Mosul on her own two feet. She needed help from one of the many houses she passed, but there was no way to know who was behind the door. Would it be another ISIS militant, or a Sunni family that would take pity on her?[29]

To this day she doesn't know why she chose the door she did. There was nothing special about it. There was no sign. But when she knocked, the family took her in. She told them her story, from the siege of Kocho to the horror of rape, and she begged them for mercy. When she was done, the father said, "Have peace in your heart. We will try to help you."[30]

Nadia made contact with her brother Hezni, who had escaped via the mountain to Iraqi Kurdistan.[31] The Sunni family helped her secure a fake ID, and the oldest son, twenty-five-year-old Nassar, accompanied her out of Mosul under the guise of husband and wife. From Mosul to Kirkuk to a refugee camp in Kurdistan, it was a long and dangerous journey. The checkpoints out of Mosul were the most harrowing. They were interrogated by militants at each one, and it took all of Nadia's strength not to collapse under their probing questions. As soon as they got to Kirkuk, Nadia took off her niqab. Finally, she could feel the breeze on her face. Finally, she was free.[32]

But it was a poor approximation of freedom. Life in the refugee camp was grueling. They lived in tents with barely enough food. They had no work and no future.[33] By some miracle, she was alive, but it wasn't much of a life. Over time, Nadia was reunited with some of her family members, including two of her sisters.[34] Their stories of escape were just as dangerous and incredible. But there were more losses, too. A mass grave near Kocho confirmed her mother's death.[35] After many failed escape attempts, her niece and best friend, Kathrine, was blown up by a bomb en route to Kurdistan.[36]

In her darkest moments, when she was too weak and terrified to sleep, Nadia fantasized about bringing her rapists and all the terrorists to justice. She imagined a great international trial where she could stand up and testify before her tormentors, where *she* could be the one with all the power. She imagined what it would feel like to visit Hajji Salman in jail, to look into his eyes and force him to remember all the horrible things he did to her.[37]

Soon, Nadia would get a chance to make that fantasy a reality.

In 2015, Nadia and one of her sisters moved to Germany, where she met fellow Yazidis who dedicated their lives to helping their brothers and sisters in Iraq. They had started an organization called Yazda to help free and support women and girls taken captive by ISIS.[38]

Meeting the founders of Yazda was a turning point. Nadia realized what her life's purpose was—to make sure no other women would suffer the way she and so many other Yazidi women had suffered. To make sure she was the last girl—the eventual title of her book—with a story like hers.[39]

In her autobiography, Nadia Murad talks about feeling powerless in captivity. Joining Yazda and speaking out changed her. It didn't erase all the bad things that had happened to her. Nothing could, of course. But slowly, she started to grow into a new person—a person who would not be silenced, a person who demanded justice.[40]

I think there was a reason God helped me escape, and a reason I met the activists with Yazda, and I don't take my freedom for granted. The terrorists didn't think that Yazidi girls would be able to leave them, or that we would have the courage to tell the world every detail of what they did to us. We defy them by not letting their crimes go unanswered. Every time I tell my story, I feel that I am taking some power away from the terrorists.[41]

Nadia told her story everywhere she could. She told it to thousands of people all across the world. She told them to open their eyes to the crimes that are happening every day and open their countries to refugees who had nowhere to go. She told them because she wanted other girls like her to know they were not alone and because she wanted the terrorists to know they did not win.[42]

It wasn't easy. Every time she told her story, she relived it. But she forced the world to relive it with her. To die a little bit each time she recounted the endless rapes. To cry with her when she found out what happened to all the people she loved. To feel the fire of justice burning in their hearts just like it burned in hers.[43]

It didn't have to be this way. After her escape to freedom, Nadia could have lived a quiet, private life. "Deciding to be honest was one of the hardest decisions I have ever made," she wrote, "and also the most important."[44] There were too many people who needed help. There were still thousands of women trapped in captivity and hundreds of thousands living in deprivation in refugee camps. There were millions of women the world over who were routinely denied the agency to control their lives.[45] Finally, she believed that healing required justice, and justice would not happen unless she made it happen.

Nadia Murad's voice made a difference. She teamed up with human rights lawyer Amal Clooney to bring the ISIS militants to justice. The first thing they had to do was make sure the evidence of ISIS's heinous crimes didn't disappear.[46] At their urging, the United Nations launched an investigation into the crimes against Yazidis and formed the Investigative Team to Promote Accountability for Crimes Committed by Da'esh/ISIL (UNITAD), which collected firsthand accounts, forensic evidence, and ISIS reports. In 2021, UNITAD recognized the atrocities committed by ISIS as genocide.[47] In November 2021, a German court convicted the first ISIS militant for crimes against humanity and genocide.[48]

Nadia was recognized for her good work. In 2016, she was named the UN's Goodwill Ambassador for the Dignity of Survivors of

Human Trafficking,[49] and in 2018, she was awarded the Nobel Peace Prize.[50] The prizes were welcome insomuch as they furthered her cause. But there was only one thing she wanted: justice.

Justice came slowly. It took several years for the United States and allied air power, along with Iraqi and Kurdish soldiers on the ground, to defeat ISIS. At the peak of its power, ISIS held about one-third of Syria and 40 percent of Iraq. In 2015, ISIS expanded its tentacles into other countries, where ISIS-affiliated terrorists carried out attacks, including at a night club in Orlando, Florida. After two years of aggressive and strategic airstrikes, Iraqi and Kurdish forces retook major cities in Iraq and Syria. In July 2017, Mosul was liberated. Other big cities followed. By December 2017, ISIS had lost 95 percent of its land.[51]

Defeating ISIS was a victory, but the five-year war had claimed many casualties. Those who survived had nowhere to go, and returning home was no homecoming. Yazidis spent generations building their lives in towns like Kocho, and ISIS militants wiped them out in an instant. They weren't just trying to kill the Yazidis; they were trying to erase their existence from history. That is the meaning of genocide.

In 2018, Nadia launched Nadia's Initiative with the goal of rebuilding what ISIS destroyed. Her organization rebuilds homes, schools, farms, health care centers, and water and electricity services.[52] For Nadia, justice has many components. Holding the terrorists accountable is one part. The other is rebuilding and reclaiming the Yazidi homeland. It is the Yazidis' way of saying, "You tried to erase us, but we will not be erased. We will not be forgotten. We are still here."

Nadia's Initiative also creates support systems for survivors of sexual assault. It empowers women by giving them access to health care, education, legal services, and emotional support. It runs a small business incubator program that trains women—many of whom had never worked outside the home—to support themselves.[53]

One such woman is Pakiza, a mother to six children, whose husband went missing shortly before 2014. After four years of living in a Kurdistan refugee camp, Pakiza and her family moved back to Sinjar City. She had no way of supporting her family until she applied to and got accepted by the initiative's incubator program. She received training and seed money to start a fabric store—the fulfillment of a lifelong dream. Not only can she provide for her family, she took control of her life.[54]

There are thousands of women like Pakiza. They are survivors. But many are broken and broke, homeless and hopeless. To this day, many still live in refugee camps surviving off the kindness of others. Many struggle with terrifying memories that haunt their waking and sleeping hours.

Nadia's Initiative is not just about survival. It is about empowerment. The difference between those two words is life-changing. Nadia knows. She is a survivor. But it wasn't until she started working with Yazda and claiming her own power that she began to live again.

Today, ISIS is largely defeated, but there is no normalcy. There are still 200,000 Yazidis displaced and living in refugee camps. There are still 2,800 women and girls missing. And there are 150,000 Yazidis who have returned to the Sinjar region, struggling to rebuild and reclaim their lives.[55] Nadia continues to be their voice.

Nadia Murad has lived through many labels in her young life. But now, eight years after her life forever changed, she has accumulated more. Goodwill ambassador. Nobel Peace Prize winner. Advocate. Fighter. Seeker of justice.

She never intended to be any of those things. She wasn't trained to give speeches. Her voice isn't unusually loud or dynamic. She is slender, and when she curls up in a ball, she looks like she could crawl inside herself. But she is powerful. She is a person people want to listen to. Her words compel leaders, presidents, and prime ministers to action. Not because anyone bestowed that power on her but because she demanded it for herself. And now she devotes her life to demanding that power for other women like her.

There are people all over the world who want to deny women their power. Some of them are truly evil—ISIS in Iraq, the ayatollahs in Iran, and the Communists in China. They crush a woman's humanity by taking away her right to think for herself and act for herself. Women are told who to marry, when to pray, and where to live. This is a global tragedy, and I'm thankful every day to live in a free country.

But even here, with all the freedom we enjoy, there are social pressures that conspire to deny women their independence. Too often, women are lumped into a box that assumes we are all the same. Too often, women are told how to dress, what to think, what to believe, what careers to pursue, when to speak, and when to smile—not by government fiat but by society's expectations.

Don't listen.

You are in charge of your life and your destiny. You don't need anyone's permission to be who you want to be. Whether it's a liberal, a conservative, a politician, a doctor, a teacher, or an at-home mom, you get to decide who you are and what you want to do with your life.

Too often, women are made out to be victims of society. In a free country like ours, we are not victims unless we choose to be. I'm not saying it's easy. But we should not fall into a trap of thinking that a woman's road to empowerment lies with someone else righting a wrong. It lies with you. You decide.

6

I grew up in Bamberg, South Carolina, a small, rural town with 2,500 people and two stop lights. You couldn't think about doing something wrong without someone telling your mom. Our schools were brick boxes. No bells or whistles. We didn't know what we didn't have. The only time we had a glimpse of finer things was if I played tennis out of town for a competition or went to a football game. We would see big, beautiful schools with beautiful tennis courts or large stadiums.

My father was a professor, my mom a social studies teacher. They instilled in me the importance of a good education. Because they were Indian parents, they emphasized certain careers. All Indian children were told they needed to become a doctor, lawyer, or engineer. I ended up becoming an accountant. I guess I was a rebel even then!

My parents left comfortable lifestyles in India to come to America, start all over, and create better lives for their children. They were only allowed to have eight dollars in their pockets when they arrived. Why would they do that? For the opportunity of the blessings of America.

I learned a lot in that small town that stays with me. The idea of neighbors helping neighbors and that people are inherently good. That I don't like bullies and I am quick to defend someone or some country that is being bullied. That it's not where you are born and raised that decides your fate but how you choose to live your life.

I remember some of my friends who lived on the other side of the tracks. Life was hard for them. Some didn't have indoor plumbing, and others relied on the food they were given to eat in school as their main meal.

When I became governor in 2011, I never forgot what it was like to grow up in a small, challenged community. My parents always taught us that the best way to appreciate God's blessings is to give back, so that's what I did. I started a nonprofit organization, which still runs today, called the Original Six Foundation. Our mission is to provide after-school programs and literacy help to the rural, challenged areas of South Carolina. We have impacted thousands of students and continue to serve.

When I began the program, someone came up to me and said, "Why are you doing this? Those people will never vote for you." I looked at him and said, "Because I used to be one of those kids." And he went silent.

I strongly believe children deserve a good education regardless of where they are born and raised. Parents of all races want the best for their children; they want their children to have a better education and better opportunities than they had.

A few years later, during my 2014 State of the State speech, I argued that it was time for South Carolina to end the educational discrimination that plagued our rural communities. This was a discrimination based not on skin color but on geography and income. Forty percent of South Carolina's students lived in rural districts, many of whom did not have even basic technological equipment and supplies. So I proposed an education plan that called for spending $177 million to upgrade rural schools, with a focus on access to technology and reading skills. The education gap in our state was a moral failing, and we had a duty to fix it.[1]

I used my position as governor to shine a light on the education gap in South Carolina. What's amazing is that there are people like Virginia Walden Ford, with no titles, no resources, and nothing but the power of their voices, willing and ready to get to work. She knew from personal experience how unfair the system was. She saw her son fall through the cracks—not because he was Black but because he lived in a poor school district filled with violence and drugs, and she didn't have the money to send him to private school.

And she was tired of it.

The cynics will tell you that one person can't make a difference, that your voice is nothing more than an echo. They are wrong. I know they are wrong because I proved the cynics wrong repeatedly. I know they're wrong because Virginia Walden Ford—a single mom who was terrified of public speaking—used her voice to fight for school choice in Washington, D.C., and changed thousands of lives for the better. She is proof of how one life can improve the lives of many.

Virginia Walden Ford

Raise Your Voice

So, what I've learned over 20 years of fighting for children and parents is that a parent's voice is incredibly powerful. And that if you can gather together people who are willing to talk about their plight in life, then you can make changes.[2]

—VIRGINIA WALDEN FORD

Our kids should never feel that they are more or less worthy based on where they live. . . . South Carolina can no longer accept the quality of our children's education being determined by where they are born and raised.[3]

—NIKKI HALEY

There are two things you need to know about Virginia Walden Ford. She would do anything for her three children, and she was terrified of public speaking. So, when her son needed her to find her voice, she didn't have a choice. She raised her voice and taught others to do the same.

This is a story about ordinary people doing extraordinary things, about the power of our voices to make small changes with huge ripple effects. This is a story about a woman who refused to take no for an answer.

Virginia Walden Ford was no stranger to adversity. She grew up in Little Rock, Arkansas, at the height of the desegregation battles. She and her twin sister were part of the second wave of Black students to desegregate Little Rock's high schools in the 1960s.[4] Only fourteen years old, she did not want to be on the front lines of this major battle, but her father told her she had a responsibility to go and do well. She had a responsibility to change the world. Even at fourteen, she believed him.[5]

A year later, she watched a large cross burn on her family's front lawn after her father was named the first Black school administrator in Little Rock. She can still see the flames dancing in her memory, smoke thick and black like the fear in her heart. Her father hugged his daughters and said, "Girls, some people do not want to see blacks do well. But change will only come if you will stand up and fight for it."[6]

Thirty-plus years later, those words became Virginia's motto as she watched her youngest son fall victim to another kind of segregation—one that separated kids based on their income and zip code. In her poor, crime-ridden neighborhood of Southeast, Washington, D.C., kids were condemned to the local public school, where metal detectors, violence, and drugs were facts of life. When kids fell through the cracks—which happened often—there was nowhere to go. Virginia and so many parents like her didn't have the money to enroll their kids in private school.[7]

The stakes were high. For some kids, it was literally life and death. A good education in a safe neighborhood could be the difference between graduating and falling into gang life, between going to college and going to jail. Virginia knew too many neighborhood kids whose lives ended before they really began. Her youngest son, William, was just eleven years old when she began to see the warning signs. She dropped him off at school, but he never made it to class. He was pulled in by drug dealers who recruited kids with expensive gifts and promised to protect them on the streets.[8] One teacher told her, "William is bad. He's a thug. I think you ought to just give up on him."[9] She didn't know what to do, but she knew she had to do *something*. She refused to give up on her son. She refused to give up, period.

So, she did the only thing she could think of. She took William out of the public school and enrolled him in a private school she could not afford. Although William had some scholarship money from a generous neighbor, Virginia still had to cover half the bill. As a single mom of three kids, that was no easy feat. So, she took a second job. She came home from her accounting job after a full day of work and went back to work at 9:00 p.m., where she did accounting and scrubbed floors for a local radio station.[10]

It was worth every penny. She noticed a difference in her son right away. He wasn't afraid to go to his new school. He wasn't afraid of being beaten up for taking an interest in his classes. He joined the track team and engaged with his teachers. For the first time in his life, there were people, other than Virginia, who took a vested interest in his academic success. He felt like he mattered, and ultimately, that was what mattered most.[11]

Even though Virginia was grateful for this unexpected opportunity, something bothered her. She knew she got lucky. Without the scholarship money, she could not afford to send William to private school. Even with it, she barely managed to pay the bills. She remembered her parents' courageous fight to integrate Arkansas's schools and give their children the same educational opportunities as white children. They accomplished their goal, but what was that education worth if the next generation of kids wasn't learning?

There had to be a better way. Virginia didn't have money, influence, or connections, but she had one thing no one could take away: her voice. She started by showing up—at school meetings with the principal, at school board meetings, and at local city council meetings.[12] At first, she was dismissed. She was told she didn't know what she was talking about, she didn't have the right information, she wasn't equipped to fight for her children.

They were wrong.

Virginia learned that nobody could fight for her child better than she could. No one else knew what it was like for her son to be trapped in a broken public school with no options. "We're the only ones who can tell stories about how our children are doing in school," she said. "What I've learned . . . is that a parent's voice is incredibly powerful."[13]

Instead of going away, she grew more persistent. She volunteered for organizations that were advocating for school choice and reached out to fellow parents and urged them to get involved. As she met more people, her story made the rounds. In 1998, House majority leader Dick Armey asked her to testify before Congress in support of a Washington, D.C., school choice bill that would give low-income D.C. families vouchers to attend private school.[14]

The 1998 fight introduced Virginia to the chaotic world of government. It was encouraging to see Democrats join with Republicans in support of the bill, but it also opened her eyes to the viciousness that infected the school choice fight. Democratic Illinois congressman Jesse Jackson Jr. called the bill a version of the "Tuskegee experiment"—a government-run study in which researchers promised to treat African Americans suffering from syphilis but instead gave them placebos and watched them suffer and die. A *Buffalo News* columnist called the proposal "a wicked little sham" that was "motivated not by love for the poor children, but by hatred of the public schools."[15] The revolting attacks shocked Virginia.

She decided the only way to combat the misinformation was to build a grassroots army. She spoke anywhere she could—community organizations, tenant association meetings, boys and girls clubs. She reached out to pastors and "community mothers"—women in Black communities who served as adoptive mothers to the neighborhood kids. She naïvely thought that people would flock to the opportunity. But so many parents were jaded by years of broken promises. Getting parents to trust her was the first hurdle. Instead of talking about policy, she told them about her personal story and struggle. She told them about William.[16]

In March 1998, she had the chance to tell her story on a much bigger stage, in public testimony before the House Committee on Education and the Workforce. It was thrilling—and terrifying. She spoke about the feeling of helplessness and hopelessness that comes from having no options. "I remember that feeling so clearly," she told the committee. "And I have heard it voiced many times from other mothers who have had nowhere to turn. . . . We know our kids, and we know what'll work best for them."[17]

After a long, hard fight, the legislation made it through both the House and the Senate. On May 8, 1998, the bill was sent to President Bill Clinton for his signature. On May 20, he vetoed the bill.[18]

Virginia felt defeated and deflated. She told her fellow advocates that she was done. She wanted nothing to do with the sordid world of government where people claimed to care about poor kids but insisted on keeping them trapped in a broken education system. She poured her anger into a *Washington Post* op-ed. "I am a lifelong Democrat," she wrote, "and I am not sure when the Democrats decided that siding with the poor and the needy is no longer part of their platform. School choice empowers parents, and I don't care who is behind it, Democrats or Republicans."[19]

But giving up wasn't in Virginia's DNA. Her father's words echoing in her memory, she founded D.C. Parents for School Choice to continue the fight for school vouchers and to serve as a resource for local parents looking for education alternatives, including charter schools.[20] She recruited parents and taught them how to tell their stories, how to fight, and how to keep at it when the naysayers tried to knock them down. For many parents, speaking up was the hardest part. She told parents, "You have every right to fight for your child to have a quality education." She told them again and again until they believed it, until they found their voices, just like she found hers. "Your voice has power," she insisted. "Just like every other American, you have a right to talk to your legislators about what you want for your child."[21]

In 2003, Virginia and her fellow advocates got another chance. The political stars aligned with Republicans controlling the House, the Senate, and the White House. Congressman Jeff Flake of Arizona introduced a D.C. school vouchers bill, and he reached out to Virginia to gather local parents for an announcement press conference.[22] Virginia delivered. On the day of the press conference, dozens of parents joined Congressman Flake and Virginia to show support for his bill.[23]

At the same time, President George W. Bush announced his intention to include $75 million in scholarship funds for low-income students in five cities, including D.C., in his 2004 budget. Later in the year, Congressmen Tom Davis and John Boehner introduced their own D.C. school vouchers bill.[24] There were minor differences between the bills, but they all shared a common purpose: to establish a scholarship fund for Washington, D.C., students in low-income households to attend the school of their choosing.

The gauntlet was thrown. Both sides dug their heels in and readied for war. D.C.'s local representative, Delegate Eleanor Norton Holmes, was a staunch opponent of school choice. When Congressman Flake introduced his bill, she declared, "If he wants a fight he will get one, a big one."[25]

Delegate Norton delivered on her promise. The teachers unions and liberal activists mobilized, lobbying congressional members to oppose the bill. The National Coalition for Public Education, comprising forty-plus different liberal organizations, sent a letter to congressional members saying, "Vouchers are neither needed nor wanted in the District of Columbia."[26]

The attacks went beyond the political arena. Raising her voice made Virginia a target. One anti-voucher newspaper lambasted Virginia and published her home address. She started receiving death threats—an eerie reminder of the night in 1967 when she and her family watched the cross burn in their front yard. Both threats were intended to terrify her, to make her feel unsafe in her own home.[27] "At times," Virginia said, "it seemed like almost everyone in a position of power opposed us, except the parents."[28]

Except the parents. Those were the key words.

They were powerless except for the power of their voices. Over time, their personal stories chafed away at the opposition. Over the course of ten months, Virginia worked closely with legislators and parents who were determined to pass this bill. She launched a petition drive to demonstrate the bill's wide public support and enthusiasm, and she organized rallies. Every day Congress was in session, Virginia made sure parents showed up on Capitol Hill wearing D.C. PARENTS FOR SCHOOL CHOICE T-shirts to speak with lawmakers and the media.[29]

The momentum shifted to their side when unlikely allies offered their support—people like D.C.'s Democratic mayor, Anthony Williams, D.C. city council education chair Kevin Chavous, and D.C. board of education president Peggy Cafritz.[30] They had all been previous opponents of school choice, but they supported the D.C. scholarship program because they had heard from too many parents who had run out of options.

"At town hall meetings, community picnics, hearings and PTA meetings, we hear the same complaints: 'I can't find the right setting for my child' or 'My child is not flourishing in this environment,'" they wrote in a *Washington Post* op-ed. "Despite steady reform, change cannot occur rapidly enough to provide relief to all public schools. As elected leaders, we cannot tell parents who yearn for an opportunity for their children to delay the same fulfillment we can provide our own children."[31]

Democratic California senator Dianne Feinstein was another unlikely ally. She had opposed vouchers for a long time, but her own story wasn't so different from those of kids like William. When she was a young girl, she switched to a private Catholic school where she was one of just a few Jewish students. On July 22, 2003, Feinstein surprised her fellow Democrats and endorsed the D.C. school choice bill. Her vote was essential to making sure the bill advanced out of the Senate Appropriations Committee.[32]

In the final push to a vote in the summer and fall of 2003, both sides ratcheted up the pressure. The parents' voices were undeniable. So was the devastating evidence. In November 2002, the D.C. superintendent issued a report showing 70 percent of D.C.'s public school students tested at or below a basic reading and math level. The average SAT score for high school seniors was 796, well below the national average of 1020. D.C. also had one of the highest dropout rates in the country.[33]

On September 5, the House of Representatives passed the bill by a slim margin of 205–203, but opponents called for a revote—allowable under House rules—when Congress returned to session on September 9. The impossibly slim margin grew slimmer still. Virginia and her fellow parents sat in the gallery watching nervously. As the minutes ticked by, the bill's supporters were running out of time. Republican leaders held the vote open an extra fifteen minutes.[34] Would this be the end of the road for them?

Not that day. The bill passed by a single vote—209–208. Only three Democrats voted for the bill. Fifteen Republicans and one Independent sided with the Democrats in opposition.[35] The bill's saving grace? During the vote, Democratic presidential candidates Representatives Dick Gephardt and Dennis Kucinich were at a Baltimore debate hosted by the Congressional Black Caucus—ironically, a group that opposed the school choice bill.[36]

One chamber down, one chamber to go. Although the bill had majority support in the Senate, Democratic senator Ted Kennedy of Massachusetts threatened to filibuster the bill. The bill needed sixty votes—and that wasn't happening. Republicans withdrew the bill in late September.[37]

But the fight wasn't over yet. The arcane world of legislative sausage-making offered supporters other weapons in their arsenal. Republicans slipped the pilot program into a large bill that controlled spending for multiple federal agencies—a common tactic because many members are reluctant to vote against spending bills that fund many of their personal priorities.

The Consolidated Appropriations Act, as it was called, ended up passing both chambers by large margins. On January 23, 2004, President Bush signed the D.C. School Choice Incentive Act into law. The final bill contained $14 million to offer $7,500 in annual scholarships to low-income students. The scholarships were part of a $40 million compromise that increased federal dollars to D.C.'s public school system.[38]

This was a historic day. At many moments throughout 2003, it seemed like the bill might fail. Congress was structured to make passing legislation inherently difficult. From committee votes to House votes to Senate votes to the White House, there are many people with the power to derail legislation along the way. Shortly after the bill was signed into law, Secretary of Education Rod Paige called the voucher program "educational emancipation"—and it was not an exaggeration. The bill offered to set thousands of D.C. students free. "Education is freedom," he said. "A good, wise, just, and compassionate country makes certain that educational opportunities are available for all of its citizens—every single one of them."[39]

For many people, this would have been the end of the story. Advocates of the bill had worked hard, pushed through the opposition, and gotten the job done. Not for Virginia. "Public policy is a marathon, not a sprint," she wrote in her memoir.

She spent the subsequent years educating parents about the scholarship program, helping them fill out application forms, and holding their hands through the process.[40]

She partnered with the Washington Scholarship Fund to recruit parents into the program. Instead of waiting for parents to come to her, she went to them. It wasn't always easy. As they ventured into D.C.'s poorest neighborhoods, many of the applicants didn't have access to a photocopier or notaries, so a member of Virginia's team became a notary public, and they brought a portable photocopier with them.[41] After everything they had been through, these obstacles were not going to get in their way.

Every day, Virginia met people who filled her heart with hope and encouragement. A drug dealer who sent the mother of his two children to apply so they wouldn't end up like him. A middle schooler who filled out the application form himself because he lived with his grandmother, who couldn't read.[42] For these families, the D.C. scholarship program was a lifesaver.

But this lifesaver could be yanked away at any moment. "Elections have consequences," Virginia writes in her book. After all, it was George W. Bush's election that made the D.C. Opportunity Scholarship Program a reality. In 2009, with Barack Obama in the White House and Democratic majorities in Congress, D.C.'s school voucher program was on the chopping block. It took the Obama administration all of three months to strip funding for the program.[43]

Virginia and her grassroots army got to work. They were part of a larger network of pro–school choice organizations, each with a role to play in this all-hands-on-deck campaign. Virginia's specialty? Putting a personal face to the fight. Just as she had in 1998 and 2003, she shone a light on the families and students who benefited from the Opportunity Scholarship Program. This fight wasn't just about numbers and data. It was about people and their stories. People like twelve-year-old Sakeithia, who was ecstatic to go to a safe school. She sent a letter to President Obama: "Dear President Obama, . . . My old public school was not a very safe place. I saw a lot of things a child should not see. I'm now learning things that were not offered to me in public school."[44]

In May 2009, Virginia helped organize a rally in D.C.'s Freedom Plaza, attended by more than one thousand parents and children. High school student Carlos Battle read a poem he wrote called "Surrender Me": "I refuse, refuse, refuse to be someone's inmate or charity case, and I'm putting all the disbelievers in their place. I'm not going to be thrown in the category of jailed or shot, I'm the new face of black youth—like it or not." After the rally, Virginia and her army marched to the office of D.C. mayor Adrian Fenty and delivered a petition signed by 7,400 D.C. residents.[45]

The day after the rally, the Obama administration offered a compromise of sorts. Students currently receiving scholarships could stay in the program through graduation, but no new students could apply.[46] Virginia and her allies were heartbroken. Throughout 2009, they upped the ante—from sit-ins outside the Department of Education to ads targeting members of Congress to public rallies. They didn't catch a break until November 2010, when the Tea Party movement swept the nation and Republicans retook control of Congress in the midterm elections.[47] Elections have consequences.

Newly elected Speaker of the House John Boehner reached out to Virginia in advance of President Obama's 2011 State of the Union speech. It was customary to fill the seats in the Capitol with special guests. But Speaker Boehner had one special type of guest in mind: D.C. Opportunity Scholarship recipients, teachers, and supporters. Shortly after the State of the Union, Boehner and longtime voucher supporter Democratic senator Joe Lieberman introduced the Scholarships for Opportunity and Results (SOAR) Act. The bill had no trouble passing the House of Representatives. The political class assumed the bill would die in the Senate, where it needed sixty votes to get past the filibuster. They were wrong.[48]

Ongoing budget negotiations between President Obama and Speaker Boehner coincided with the school choice fight. Barring an agreement, the federal government would run out of money at midnight on April 9, 2011. On April 8, the two reached a deal, and Boehner had insisted on including the D.C. Opportunity Scholarship Program in the final agreement.[49]

Great moments are not always measurable. That is not the case here. Since 2004, more than 11,177 children have received an education through the D.C. scholarship program.[50] That's 11,177 children who got a second chance in school and life. That's 11,177 children who didn't get sucked into gangs, fall through the cracks of a broken system, or drop out of school. That's 11,177 children who will go on to bigger and better things. That's 11,177 children whose lives were changed because one woman found the courage to raise her voice.

There were a lot of people who played important roles in the school choice fight in Washington, D.C. Many of them were important. Many of them had titles and the media on speed dial. But Virginia Walden Ford was able to make an impact because she had none of the trappings of importance. Her strength lay in the passion of her personal story. She quickly learned—and her opponents never did—that there is great power in the everyday stories of ordinary people. She lifted her voice up, and it quickly became two voices, then three, then four. Soon, she had an army of ordinary voices. Together, they weren't so ordinary anymore.

Too often I meet people who discount the power of their own voices. "I'm not important," they tell me. "No one will listen." With all due respect, they're wrong. Your voice is the most powerful weapon you have. When you use it in the right way, you can move hearts, change minds, and make a difference.

Sure, some people will try to talk over you. Don't let them. Some people with argue with you. Good. You can persuade them. Whatever you do, don't ever underestimate the power of your voice.

7

Over the spring and summer of 2020, I watched America burn. From Minneapolis to New York to Seattle to Portland to Philadelphia to Washington, D.C., rioters used the mantle of Black Lives Matter to destroy American cities, businesses, and lives.

It was heartbreaking knowing the wave of violence would do nothing to improve civil rights in America. Angry mobs and shattered cities are not what America is about.

The America I know and love is very different than the chaos, destruction, and anger that took place. The America I know allowed a brown girl with Indian parents to become the first female minority governor in the country. The America I know is marked by mistakes, yes, but also incredible, awe-inspiring progress. America is not perfect, but the principles of freedom and opportunity that gave birth to our country are perfect. Our American story is about constantly striving to live up to those principles and achieving amazing success in doing so.

When I delivered my first inaugural speech as governor of South Carolina in 2011, I quoted columnist George Will, who wrote about the occasion, "If the question is which state has changed most in the last half century, the answer might be California. But if the question is which state has changed most for the better, the answer might be South Carolina."[1]

The history of the Confederate flag in South Carolina is an example of this. First raised over the state capitol dome in 1961, the flag was the source of much debate. Growing up, I knew people who viewed the flag as a matter of history and Southern heritage. I also knew people for whom the flag was a constant and painful reminder of slavery. In 2000, both sides reached a compromise to move the flag from the capitol dome to a monument honoring Confederate soldiers right in front of the statehouse.[2]

By the time I became governor ten years later, many people in our state had moved on. We were focused on bringing jobs to South Carolina and fixing our schools. That changed on Wednesday, June 17, 2015—a day I will never forget. An avowed white supremacist walked into a Bible study class at the historic Emanuel African Methodist Episcopal Church (often called Mother Emanuel) in Charleston and murdered nine African Americans during Bible study, including the pastor, over the course of six minutes.

The pain and tragedy of the Mother Emanuel shooting brought the flag to the forefront. It begged the question of why we still had the Confederate flag flying on the statehouse grounds.

In the wake of this gruesome tragedy, South Carolina came together. We didn't have riots. We held vigils. We didn't have protests. We had hugs. Instead of hatred, we offered comfort. This tragedy called for prayer and healing, and the people of South Carolina rose to the moment. There was a place for the Confederate flag, but that was not at the statehouse but a museum. So, that's what we did. The bill to remove the flag from the statehouse grounds passed both chambers of the legislature by a two-thirds majority, and I signed it into law. Republicans and Democrats, Blacks and whites—we moved forward together and left our past in the past.

This was a small example of progress in South Carolina's—and America's—story. It is proof of America's inherent goodness and potential. Claudette Colvin and civil rights heroes like her are even greater examples. Claudette refused to give up her seat on a Montgomery city bus because she knew she had constitutional rights regardless of her skin color. She was not violent or disrespectful. Rosa Parks's act of protest would not happen until nine months later.

We honor these heroes' legacies by striving to do better—not by tearing down our history and uprooting statues of Abraham Lincoln and George Washington but by learning the lessons and adding to our history. From Martin Luther King Jr. to Rosa Parks, civil rights leaders inspired so many because they believed in the promise of America, and they wanted every citizen to enjoy that promise equally.

America is about opportunity for all citizens—regardless of race, gender, or circumstances—to work hard and make a life for themselves and their families. This is the story of a young, courageous girl who had the vision of what America should be. This story is not well-known, but it should be.

Claudette Colvin

Stand for What's Right
Even If You're Standing Alone

It felt like Sojourner Truth was on one side pushing me down, and Harriet Tubman was on the other side of me pushing me down. I couldn't get up.[3]

—CLAUDETTE COLVIN

Courage doesn't come from doing what everybody says. Courage comes from doing what you know is right.

—NIKKI HALEY

Before there was Rosa Parks, there was Claudette Colvin. The world-famous story about a Black woman's refusal to give up her seat for a white passenger on a Montgomery, Alabama, bus was not without precedent. The same story happened nine months earlier, except the Black woman was a girl.

She was fifteen years old.

Claudette Colvin was a junior in high school when she made history. She was a girl who knew her own worth. She was also a hero ahead of her time. She never became a celebrated icon like other civil rights activists, but that doesn't make her story any less important. In some ways, it makes it more important.

Her story starts in the Jim Crow South. Born in 1939, she was raised in a world of "separate but equal"—the 1896 Supreme Court ruling that gave a legal stamp of approval to segregation. Except it was anything but equal.

Alabama was ground zero for segregation and the civil rights battles of the 1950s and 1960s. After all, Montgomery was the Confederacy's first capital city (later moved to Richmond, Virginia) and home to the inauguration of Jefferson Davis, the president of the Confederacy.[4] Montgomery was also home to Martin Luther King Jr.'s Dexter Avenue church and the famous bus boycott.

Claudette Colvin went to an all-Black elementary school in rural Pine Level, Alabama, that had just one room for all six grades.[5] When her family moved to Montgomery, she attended one of the city's two segregated high schools, where they didn't have enough money for books and desks.[6] There were separate neighborhoods, movie theaters, elevators, water fountains, bathrooms, and, of course, there was separate seating on the city buses. There were also many rules about what Black people could do. They could walk through the beautiful, historic local park, but they couldn't play ball or sit on the benches. They could shop in the white department stores, but they couldn't try anything on. Claudette's mother traced the outline of her foot on a piece of paper before they went shoe shopping and matched the shoes to the outline.[7]

Claudette was smart and curious, and she asked a lot of questions. "Why don't the stars fall? Where is Japan? Shouldn't Easter be on a Monday?" But one question haunted her throughout her formative years: How did white people come to rule over Black people? She didn't understand how God could create different types of people with different levels of worth. When she was just a child, she told her pastor, "I don't want to serve a God that would have a cursed race."[8]

As a high school student, Claudette continued to see injustice everywhere she looked. There was a racial hierarchy even at her all-Black high school. The most popular, beautiful, and desired girls were light-skinned and had straight, flowing hair. Some girls spent hours trying to coax their thick locks to look more "white." Claudette had no luck in either department. Her skin was very dark, and her coarse hair was stubborn.[9]

"For some reason we seemed to hate ourselves," Claudette said. "We students put down our hair texture and skin color all the time. Can you imagine getting up in the morning every day and looking in the mirror and saying to yourself, 'I have bad hair?' "[10]

All that changed for Claudette when her favorite teacher, Miss Geraldine Nesbitt, entered her life. Formally a literature teacher, Miss Nesbitt wanted to teach her students about life. They read great books, but they also read the Magna Carta, the Constitution, and the Articles of Confederation. They discussed Black history and leaders like Harriet Tubman and Sojourner Truth. Perhaps most importantly, Miss Nesbitt challenged her students to see themselves as worthy of love and acceptance. "There's no such thing as 'good hair'—hair is just hair," she said. "Everyone is born with the hair they have and you just do the best you can with it."[11]

In February 1955, Miss Nesbitt teamed up with Claudette's history teacher to teach the class about Negro History Week. Throughout the month, Claudette immersed herself in her history and her rights as an American. The injustices in Montgomery took on a new light. "I was tired of adults complaining about how badly they were treated and not doing anything about it," she said. Claudette wanted to do something that mattered.[12]

That February prepared Claudette for her history-making moment. The emotional fire had always been there. Now, thanks to people like Miss Nesbitt, she was intellectually ready. She knew what she believed in. She knew what her rights were. She knew she had to stand up for them or no one else would.

The Montgomery bus lines epitomized the injustice of the Jim Crow South. In other Southern cities, the rules were simple. Whites sat in the front and Blacks sat in the back, meeting up in the middle but always separate. That was humiliating enough. But the rules in Montgomery were different. They were worse.[13]

Montgomery buses had thirty-six seats. The first four rows contained ten seats and were saved for whites only. Even when the bus was completely empty, Black passengers were not allowed to sit in the first four rows. The remaining twenty-six seats were at the discretion of the driver. At any time, he could order Black passengers to give up their seats for white passengers. Even old, pregnant, and handicapped passengers were not given a pass. None of that mattered. The only thing that mattered was the color of their skin.[14]

When the bus pulled up to a stop, all passengers entered through the front door to pay their bus fare, but that's where the similarities ended. White passengers continued on to their seats. Unless the first four rows were empty, Black passengers had to get off the bus and reboard through the rear door. Sometimes, the driver pulled away before the passengers had a chance to reenter. Why? Because he could.[15]

For Blacks, riding the Montgomery bus system

meant getting yelled at and standing constantly. Standing in the heat. Standing on tired feet at the end of a long day. Standing with bags and children demanding attention. Standing all the while knowing Blacks paid the same fare as whites and got separate and unequal treatment.

On Wednesday, March 2, 1955, separate and unequal met its match. After school, fifteen-year-old Claudette Colvin got out of school for an early dismissal day and waited with her friends for the bus at the corner of Dexter Avenue and Bainbridge Street, just like she always did. When it pulled up, she showed her half-fare student coupon to the driver and walked straight to the back since there were no whites seated yet. She took a window seat near the rear door with three schoolmates filling out the rest of the row. Over several blocks, the bus filled up. White passengers quickly occupied the first four rows. Soon, there were no empty seats, and the aisle filled with standing passengers.[16]

It didn't take long for the driver to look in Claudette's direction and yell, "I need those seats!" The other girls got up and moved to the back to stand. Claudette froze. Memories of everything she learned the month before came rushing to the forefront. She had rights—that much she knew.[17] She said to herself, "This is my time to take a stand for justice."[18]

There were now three empty seats in Claudette's

row and plenty of room for the white woman to sit, but she refused so long as Claudette remained seated. It dawned on Claudette that this was the whole point of segregation—to show that Blacks were "behind" whites. A white woman sitting in the same row as a Black teenager would send the message that they were all the same.[19]

Which is exactly why Claudette didn't budge.

Soon, the driver pulled over by a waiting squad car. Two Montgomery police officers boarded the bus and told Claudette to rise. She didn't move. She started crying and said, "It's my constitutional right to sit here as much as that lady. I paid my fare, it's my constitutional right!"[20]

The cops grabbed her by her hands and dragged her off the bus. Her books flew through the air, but she didn't fight back. She went limp and continued to say, "It's my constitutional right!"[21]

And that's how fifteen-year-old Claudette Colvin found herself sitting in the back of a police car, handcuffed with tears streaming down her face. Throughout the ride, the cops belittled her, called her names, and tried to guess her bra size. Then, they drove her to the city jail and dropped her in a cell.[22]

She broke down in tears again and prayed "like I had never prayed before."[23] Decades later, she still remembers the sound of the cell door clanging shut.[24]

Claudette's mother came with their pastor and bailed her out, but that was just the beginning of her ordeal. Claudette had stood up to a white bus driver and two white police officers. She challenged the ruling order in Montgomery. And she did it as a fifteen-year-old Black girl in 1955. That was the kind of thing that could get a person killed.[25]

Her family and neighbors stayed up all night keeping watch for the Ku Klux Klan. Claudette was terrified. But she was also proud. On the drive home, Reverend Johnson told her something that stayed with her. "Claudette, I'm so proud of you. Everyone prays for freedom. We've all been praying and praying. But you're different—you want your answer the next morning. And I think you just brought the revolution to Montgomery."[26]

Claudette's story spread like wildfire. She quickly became known as "the girl who got arrested." Some of her schoolmates and teachers applauded her courage. Others were nervous. They worried that Claudette's brazenness was going to make life harder for everyone—and it was already hard enough. And some people were embarrassed. Why did a fifteen-year-old high school student have the courage that so many adults lacked?[27]

Claudette's parents enlisted Fred Gray to take her case. Only twenty-four years old and six months out of law school, Gray was one of Montgomery's two Black lawyers. Like Claudette, he had grown up in Montgomery and breathed in the city's injustices like a toxin. He promised himself he would go to college, get a law degree, and return to Montgomery to fight for civil rights. And that's exactly what he did.[28]

When Claudette's case was presented to him, he saw an opportunity. He was eager for a test case to argue that Montgomery's bus laws were unconstitutional. This was the first chance he'd gotten. Every other passenger who had violated the bus rules ended up pleading guilty and paying the fine. Fifteen-year-old Claudette was the first to plead not guilty.[29]

On March 18, 1955, Claudette and her parents headed to Montgomery's juvenile court. She was charged with three crimes: breaking the city's segregation laws, disturbing the peace, and assaulting a police officer. The city's lawyer introduced a letter from a white witness saying Claudette had been violent while the police officers were the picture of Southern gentleness. Fred Gray presented Black witnesses who told the opposite story. It didn't matter. Judge Hill quickly issued his ruling: guilty of all three charges.[30] The next morning, the *Montgomery Advertiser* newspaper declared, NEGRO GUILTY OF VIOLATION OF CITY BUS SEGREGATION LAWS. The article added that "a bus driver has police power while in charge and must see that white and Negro passengers are segregated."[31]

Montgomery's Black community was furious. Civil rights leaders debated launching a citywide bus boycott. But some felt Claudette was not the right face for the movement. She was too young, too "emotional," too "feisty." Her parents (really her great-aunt and great-uncle) were too working-class and not part of the right social circles.[32]

Nine months later, on December 1, 1955, Rosa Parks refused to give up her bus seat for a white passenger. She was arrested, fingerprinted, and released on bond. Parks was a seamstress by day and was active with Montgomery's branch of the National Association for the Advancement of Colored People (NAACP.) She was well respected and well behaved. The Montgomery civil rights community had found its face.[33]

The next day, an anonymous pamphlet calling for a one-day bus boycott made its way throughout the Black community. It read, "Another Negro woman has been arrested and thrown in jail because she refused to get up out of her seat on the bus for a white person to sit down. It is the second time since the Claudette Colvin case. . . . Please stay off all buses Monday." The morning of Monday, December 5, the streets of Montgomery were quiet and empty. The Black community got the message. The boycott was official.[34]

What started as a one-day boycott became a 381-day movement. It required tremendous effort and planning to arrange alternate transportation for thousands of Montgomery's Black workers and students. Run by Martin Luther King Jr. and others, the Montgomery Improvement Association developed an elaborate and voluntary carpool system that shepherded Montgomery's Black community all over the city. It even took up collections to pay for the cost of gasoline.[35]

It didn't take long for the city to feel the effects of the boycott. City Lines bus company was hemorrhaging $3,200 a day and had to lay off drivers. The segregationists got desperate. Mayor W. A. "Tacky" Gayle sicced the police on carpool drivers to harass them. Bombs were lobbed at Black homes and churches. Both sides dug their heels in, and some people wondered how the standoff would end.[36]

Fred Gray had an idea. Two years earlier, the U.S. Supreme Court had invalidated "separate but equal" in education under the landmark case *Brown v. Board of Education.* In a unanimous decision, nine Justices ruled segregation in America's schools was unconstitutional. Shouldn't the same legal reasoning apply to Montgomery's bus system?[37]

Gray filed his case challenging the constitutionality of Alabama's bus laws with the federal court in Alabama. He found five plaintiffs (one eventually dropped out) willing to sign on to the case. The youngest was a name he knew well: Claudette Colvin.[38]

When Fred Gray showed up at the Colvins' home and asked Claudette if she would be part of the case, she didn't hesitate. He reminded her of the risks. The threats. The violence. She understood, but she wouldn't let fear get in the way. "You had to do what you had to do," she said.[39]

Three months later, on May 11, Claudette walked up the steps of the Montgomery courthouse. It was the 159th day of the Montgomery bus boycott, and the segregationists showed no sign of relenting. Just the opposite. On February 21, more than one hundred Black activists were indicted for violating a 1921 law that banned boycotts "without just or legal cause." The targets included Martin Luther King Jr., many Black ministers, and the voluntary carpool drivers. This fight was far from over.[40]

Fred Gray saved Claudette's testimony for last. When it was her turn, she told her story from beginning to end. She talked about being dragged off the bus, handcuffed, and thrown into an adult prison. She talked about how it felt to be treated like a dog.[41]

After the hearing, the three federal judges went to a back room and deliberated for ten minutes. Two judges voted in favor of the plaintiffs, one in favor of the city. Judges Johnson and Rivers wrote in their majority opinion that the segregation laws on Alabama's buses violated the Fourteenth Amendment. "The 'separate but equal' doctrine set forth by the Supreme Court in 1896 in the case of *Plessy v. Ferguson* can no longer be applied."[42]

Montgomery's Black community rejoiced, but their celebrations were quickly put on hold. Mayor Gayle announced he was appealing the decision to the U.S. Supreme Court. As the case awaited its fate in Washington, the boycott continued and the violence intensified. Hate mail, threatening phone calls, and the occasional bomb in a front yard were all part of regular life in Montgomery. But on November 13, 1956, the Supreme Court affirmed the lower court's decision in *Browder v. Gayle*. Jim Crow was officially over on Alabama's buses.[43]

Browder v. Gayle never became famous the way *Brown v. Board of Education* or other civil rights cases did. Fame is a finicky thing. It has a lot to do with timing and luck. It is not always an accurate measure of importance and impact. Claudette Colvin knew that better than anyone.

Claudette is a hero, but for so long, she was an unsung hero. She stood up to injustice even though she stood alone. She was the first to defy Montgomery's bus laws and the first to refuse to give in. There is a terrifying solitude in being the first. History is not always kind to firsts. Some are rejected, disdained, and forgotten.

Claudette experienced a little of all three. After the court case, she needed money and a job, but no one wanted to hire her. She was too recognizable. After all, she was "the girl who got arrested," and that came with risks. Alabama's buses might have been integrated, but racial tensions didn't disappear overnight. In the immediate aftermath of *Browder v. Gayle*, violence spread through Montgomery. People were scared, and they didn't want to be associated with troublemakers who might make them a target. Claudette ended up moving to New York so she could make a living.[44] For a long time, she was a blip in the history books.

But that didn't mean she didn't make a difference. Before she stood her ground, the Black community in Montgomery had focused on measured steps and compromises. The local civil rights groups met with city officials with a proposal to make Montgomery's bus laws more like those of other Jim Crow Southern cities.[45] They didn't even broach the idea of eliminating segregation. They were looking for baby steps. Along came Claudette Colvin to show everyone another way. Nine months later, Rosa Parks finished what Claudette started.

Claudette's courage changed the course of history. She stood up when no one else would.

She made a scene when too many people wanted to play by the rules. She forced the adults to look in the mirror and ask themselves why they weren't taking the same stand, to answer the question: Why was Claudette Colvin standing alone?

There were plenty of civil rights heroes, and they all deserve credit for their contributions. But when it comes to fighting for the simple dignity of being able to sit wherever she wanted on a city bus, Claudette Colvin was the first in Montgomery. "I don't mean to take anything away from Mrs. Parks," Fred Gray said, "but Claudette gave all of us the moral courage to do what we did."[46]

In February 2005, Claudette returned home to Montgomery, Alabama, to speak to students at Booker T. Washington Magnet High School. A lot of time had passed since the day she took a stand, but the memories were fresh in her mind. Her message was simple: "Don't give up. Keep struggling, and don't slide back."[47]

Decades after the fact, Claudette regrets nothing about her youthful rebellion. She knows that change doesn't happen by sitting on the sidelines. The path to justice can be slow and painful. There is no shortcut to righting wrongs, no easy way out. Sometimes, you just have to pick your head up and soldier on. Sometimes, doing the right thing can be lonely. Remind yourself that you are not really alone. All over the world, there are people like Claudette Colvin standing up for what's right.

As United Nations ambassador, I saw what happens when countries are too afraid to speak out. They refused to denounce the most brutal human rights violations in Cuba and Venezuela for fear of angering China or Russia or jeopardizing trade relationships. They didn't want to make enemies, and they didn't want to be singled out. The result? They did nothing, and nothing changed.

The world needs its Rosa Parkses. But it also desperately needs its Claudette Colvins. We need the unsung heroes, the young, adventurous fighters who have the courage to show the world the right direction.

In 2021, at age eighty-two, Claudette was still fighting. Although her case was appealed and two out of the three charges were dropped, she was never taken off probation. Whenever she returned to Alabama to visit family, there was always a lurking fear that if she said the wrong thing or looked at someone the wrong way, the police would come for her.[48]

It had taken her sixty-seven years, but it was time for her to take another stand. She returned to Montgomery with her lawyer—ninety-year-old Fred Gray—by her side with a petition to clear her record. The Montgomery district attorney agreed. "I guess you can say that now I am no longer a juvenile delinquent," Colvin joked.[49]

Of course, she was always so much more than that. She was exactly what the country needed.

8

When President Trump asked me to be his ambassador to the United Nations, I would only agree based on a few conditions. It needed to be a cabinet position because I wanted to report directly to the president. I wanted a seat on the National Security Council so I was in the room when decisions were made. And I told him, "I'm not going to be a wallflower or a talking head. I need to be able to say what I think."

I stipulated these conditions because I wanted to do a good job for the president and for my country. Part of taking on a challenge is setting yourself up for success. I didn't want to let the president or my country down.

To President Trump's credit, he replied, "That's exactly why I want you to do this!"

True to my word, I didn't hold back from saying what needed to be said at the United Nations. I believed—and President Trump agreed—that the United States' role at the United Nations had been marked by weakness and capitulation during the Obama administration, and it was time to right the ship. As I told the press on my first day at UN headquarters, "Our goal with the administration is to show value at the United Nations, and the way that we'll show value is to show our strength, show our voice, have the backs of our allies, and make sure our allies have our back as well."[1]

It wasn't just at the United Nations. I was honest with the president about my opinions and recommendations, and I told him when I supported him and when I disagreed with him. And when other members of the administration tried to tell me whom to hire or force me to do things their way, I stood firm. President Trump didn't ask me to join his administration to be a mindless bureaucrat. I had a job to do, and I needed to do it in the way I thought was best. And true to his word, President Trump had my back.

Things really came to a head when the president decided to make good on his promise to move the American embassy in Israel from Tel Aviv to Jerusalem. Not only did most of the United Nations oppose this change but many of the president's national security team did as well. I agreed with the president, and I told him so. Every country should have the right to decide where to base its embassy, and Israel's embassy needed to be in the capital—Jerusalem.

Service shouldn't mean blindly following instructions. If I had done that, I would have been doing my country and the president a disservice. My job called for leadership and strength. That was the only way for America to regain the respect of the other countries and get things done. Being a yes-woman might have made some people's jobs easier, but it wouldn't help the United States or our allies.

Some people think women in leadership shouldn't rock the boat. They find it uncomfortable or out of place. Well, that's their problem. Not ours. Leadership means doing what's right even if you have to rock the boat.

Virginia Hall's story is incredible. She never stopped trying to serve her country even after she was rejected multiple times. When she finally got an opportunity to serve, she didn't shy away from doing the best job she knew how—and that meant speaking up and speaking out.

As a spy for British and American intelligence agencies during World War II, she was often charged with reporting to less qualified superiors. She refused to follow their orders when those orders would have endangered her life or the lives of her recruits. When she was told a particular mission wasn't possible, she didn't take no for an answer. She found a way. Virginia Hall was one of the most important players in the French Resistance against Nazi Germany at a time when there were almost no women in military intelligence. She was also one of the most knowledgeable and skilled recruits on the ground in France. Refusing to disagree and speak up would have been a tragedy.

Service requires giving of yourself, but it doesn't mean losing yourself. Great leaders have the courage and wisdom to know when to follow orders and when to push back. Virginia Hall was a truly great leader. She demanded the opportunity to prove her worth. She demanded to be listened to and respected. She demanded to be trusted. But she never demanded honors, titles, or recognition. She rarely spoke about her accomplishments, even when pressed. As a result, it took decades for historians to unearth her story. It's an amazing story that needs to be told.

Virginia Hall

Service over Self

I must have liberty, with as large a charter as I please.[2]

—VIRGINIA HALL

I'm not going to be a wallflower or a talking head. I need to be able to say what I think.

—NIKKI HALEY

Virginia Hall was running for her life. More accurately, she was climbing.

As she fled Nazi-controlled France for Spain by foot, she climbed five thousand feet through the snowy Pyrenees Mountains. The higher she climbed, the icier and colder it got. The wind was brutal, the snow was deep, and slipping would spell certain death with steep drop-offs on both sides.[3]

When she reached a pass at six thousand feet, the guide let her and her fellow hikers rest. She nibbled on what little food she had and sent a radio message to London that read, "Cuthbert is being tiresome, but I can cope." The receiving officer messaged back, "If Cuthbert is tiresome, have him eliminated."[4]

Of course, the receiving officer had no idea that Cuthbert was the nickname Virginia Hall gave to her prosthetic leg, and eliminating "him" was not an option.

This is the incredible story of Virginia Hall, who rejected a comfortable life in America to do something important. At the time, she had no idea just how important a role she would play or just how much she would matter. Or even how hard she would have to fight just to have a shot at making a difference.

Virginia Hall became one of the most important spies of the Allied effort in World War II. She was brave, selfless, and ahead of her time. She had always wanted to serve her country but was regularly denied. When British intelligence officers were desperate for recruits willing to go behind enemy lines, they took a chance on a disabled woman. Virginia was happy to take advantage of their desperation.

The life of undercover missions and daring escapes was not the life her mother imagined for little Virginia. Born to well-to-do parents in Baltimore in 1906, Virginia's childhood should have been a clue that she was not the sort of person to go along with convention. She did all the things girls were *not* supposed to do at the turn of the century: hunting, skinning rabbits, riding bareback, and wearing a bracelet made out of live snakes. Her mother hoped Virginia would marry one of the wealthy boys who chased after her and settle down. Virginia had other ideas. In 1924, she wrote in her high school yearbook, "I must have liberty."[5]

Liberty was not part of her mother's plan.

After graduating high school, Virginia was engaged for a brief period, but that didn't last long. Thanks to family trips to Europe and a gift for languages, she loved traveling. She wanted to meet people, see the world, and be a diplomat. Her mother was appalled, but her father supported her while she went to university[6]—to Radcliffe (Harvard's women's school) in Cambridge, Massachusetts; Barnard College in New York City; then to Paris, Vienna, Strasbourg, Grenoble, and Toulouse.[7]

She spent three years hopping across Europe, becoming proficient in five languages, falling in love with France, and watching Europe change before her eyes as Mussolini turned Italy into a one-party state and Hitler's National Socialist Party gathered steam in Germany. She returned home to America with a dream of joining the Foreign Service, even though few positions were available to women. She was rejected.[8]

She found life back home stifling, so she took a secretarial job at the American embassy in Warsaw, Poland, but tired of it before too long.

Soon, she was off to Turkey in 1933, but found the tasks waiting for her just as mundane as those of her previous job. A few months in Turkey, though, would set the course for the rest of her life.[9]

Turkey was a wonderful place for an outdoor adventurer like Virginia. On one of her regular hunting trips, she slipped trying to climb over a fence. Her gun dropped and she accidentally shot herself in the foot at close range. An infection took hold, and her leg became gangrenous. She was twenty-seven years old when the doctors in Turkey cut off her left leg to save her life.[10]

When she woke up, Virginia was devastated. For a free-spirited young woman, losing her leg was like a death sentence. The next couple of nights were spent in and out of consciousness and in tremendous pain, until she saw a vision—as she described it—of her dead father urging her to be strong and survive. So, that's exactly what she did.[11]

With her father's words echoing in her brain, she got a prosthetic leg and learned to walk again. Weighing eight pounds and often rubbing against her skin, the wooden leg and metal foot was both a blessing and a burden she would struggle with throughout her life. Sad as she was, she refused to sit around and stew about her lot. As soon as she could travel, she was off to Venice, Italy, where she took a job at the American consulate and learned a valuable lesson in self-reliance. She learned to get around Venice's famous bridges and steps—an architectural detail that was not kind to a new amputee—by buying her own gondola. She learned to solve problems. She learned to hide her limp and her pain—both the physical and the emotional. And she learned to read the political tea leaves as the world around her descended into violent extremes.[12]

Virginia wanted to do more. In 1937, she tried one last time to win a diplomatic post with the U.S. State Department but was rejected due to her disability (or so the State Department claimed). She even appealed to President Franklin Roosevelt through family friends to no avail. The State Department sent her to Estonia for more clerical work until she had enough. In the spring of 1939, she quit.[13]

A few months later, on September 1, 1939, Germany invaded Poland, and the war clouds opened over Europe. Since America was not interested in her services, she went to Great Britain, where she applied to the female arm of the British Army. She was rejected—again—due to being a foreigner. She went to Paris and took the only job she could get—driving ambulances for the French Ninth Artillery Regiment. In May 1940, Germany invaded France, and Virginia watched in horror as the French military and government collapsed like a poorly baked soufflé. Wouldn't anyone stand up to the growing specter of totalitarianism?[14]

It turns out, Britain had launched a new espionage agency called the Special Operations Executive (SOE) in the summer of 1940, with the hopes of infiltrating France, providing the British Army with invaluable intelligence, and sabotaging the Nazi enemy. The problem? Few men wanted to sign up for such a dangerous mission. When SOE officials chanced upon Virginia, many opposed signing up a woman, but in some ways she was the ideal candidate. As an American and a woman, she could get around Nazi-occupied France more easily than most. Fluent in the French language and customs, she could establish crucial on-the-ground relationships. On April 1, 1941, she began her new job and spent nearly five months in training. She learned how and when to eliminate a target, how to pick locks, how to withstand a Gestapo (Nazi secret police) interrogation, and how to hide microfilm. On August 23, 1941, she was dispatched to Paris.[15]

She had no idea what was in store for her, but she knew it was far better than anything she had done until then.

Virginia entered Paris under the guise of an American journalist for the *New York Post*, writing such articles as EXCLUSIVE: BATHROOM OFFICES IN VICHY: REPORTER

FINDS CAPITAL CROWDED. These articles were more than her playing a part; they allowed Virginia to include important details about everyday life in occupied France for her fellow agents back in London until she could establish a means of communication.[16]

Over the next few months, Virginia adapted to her new role. She moved to Lyon in France's "free zone," which was under the German-allied Vichy French government's jurisdiction instead of the Nazis'. She developed a network of recruits consisting of a colorful cast of characters united by a desire to free France and defeat the Nazis. There was the flamboyant owner of a well-trafficked brothel, the conniving gynecologist who enjoyed infecting his German clients with syphilis or gonorrhea, a perfume maker, hairdressers, factory owners, and many more. Virginia even managed to infiltrate the Gestapo in France so she would be warned in case of a leak.[17]

It was lonely, fearful work. Even though Virginia was traveling and meeting people constantly, life as a spy required a bubble of solitude. Trust no one completely. Don't be careless. Don't get emotional. Tragedy forced her to learn those lessons well before the war, hiding the truth about her leg and her pangs of disappointment, building façades, and doing what her father's ghost had told her to do—survive.[18]

On December 7, 1941, Japan bombed Pearl Harbor, and the United States officially entered World War II. Being an American no longer protected Virginia. It made her a target. France was growing more dangerous by the day. The Vichy government was officially neutral, but in reality its alliance with Hitler grew, as did its cruelty. It was common for the government to conduct random raids and deliver hundreds of people to the Nazis. The *New York Post* begged Virginia to come home as her assignment had become too dangerous. She refused.[19]

The winter of 1942 was cold and cruel. Loneliness and fear weighed on Virginia in a physical way. A fellow agent showed up at her hotel room one night in a state of panic, warning that her life was in danger thanks to a betrayal by a double agent. Still, Virginia refused to leave. She had built up a vast network of hundreds of men and women who could be counted on to provide information, house agents, deliver messages and supplies, and perform other important activities. She was so effective that the German officials wondered who was the cunning "man" who orchestrated the Resistance in France.[20]

The danger grew, and Virginia took precautions. She changed her alias several times. She moved from her hotel room to an apartment. But despite the steady barrage of warnings, she refused to desert her post because she had a new and even more dangerous mission on her to-do list: break out twelve SOE agents from the French prison.[21]

The plan was as elaborate as it was creative. She managed to smuggle in food and fresh clothing to the prisoners that contained all the basic materials to file down a metal key to their jail cell. She arranged transportation and safe houses to hide the agents after the escape. And she hatched a plan to move the prisoners over the mountains to Spain and eventually to England. But Virginia and her cohorts still needed a way to communicate with the prisoners on the inside. They found their answer in a seventy-year-old French priest who managed to smuggle in a "piano"—also known as a radio transmitter.[22]

When the day of the escape finally came, everything had to go exactly right. The guards and other inmates were bought off, distracted, or put to sleep with a sedative. The makeshift key creaked a little too loudly but still worked. The twelve men pried open the barbed wire with their makeshift tools, crawled out, ran several miles to a waiting truck, and hopped in. As the Vichy police and Gestapo searched for the missing prisoners, Virginia's ragtag team of prostitutes and doctors spread misleading rumors about a British plane picking up the prisoners.[23]

In reality, the prisoners were deposited in the countryside, where they walked until they reached an old barn that served as their home for two weeks. In small groups, the men met up with Virginia in Lyon, where she prepared them for their final escape. Eventually, all twelve found safety in London, in what the SOE historian called "one of the war's most useful operations of the kind." So great were Virginia's escapades that the SOE submitted her name for the title of Commander of the Most Excellent Order of the British Empire—one of Britain's highest civilian honors. Once again, she was rejected, probably because it would have ruffled too many feathers. A woman overseeing major intelligence and paramilitary operations was still a bitter pill for many Brits to swallow.[24]

The Germans were furious and redoubled their efforts to find the person responsible. They had narrowed their targets to an English or Canadian woman with a limp who went by the name Marie Monin. With her impeccable sixth sense, Virginia could feel the enemy closing in on her.[25]

It all came crumbling down when a French priest looking for a shortcut to riches offered his espionage services to the Nazis. Robert Alesch used anti-Nazi sermons to win over members of the Resistance in his church and exploited their allegiance to learn the right code words and people to approach to get close to Virginia. Soon, Alesch was on the inside, acting as one of the most devious double agents in France. The Germans were ecstatic. They had finally found the "Limping Lady."[26]

Virginia sensed her time in France was coming to an end. She didn't know Alesch had compromised her, but she knew her address had been handed over to the Germans. She knew she was being watched. On Sunday, November 8, 1942, Allied troops landed in German-controlled North Africa in Operation Torch—the beginning of a larger plan for the Allied forces to invade southern Europe. Soon, all of France would be under Hitler's control. Virginia caught the last train to southern France, a three-hundred-mile journey that deposited her twenty miles from the Spanish border. But there was only one way out of France, and that was over the mountains.[27]

That's how Virginia Hall found herself climbing through the Pyrenees, annoyed with Cuthbert, and wondering if she would make it to the other side. It would have been an incredible physical feat for an able-bodied person with two healthy legs to make this climb. For Virginia, it was a miracle. It was a testament not just to her physical endurance but also to her mental fortitude as well.[28]

By now, the Germans were clamoring for her head. Wanted posters with her likeness spread across France with the words, THE ENEMY'S MOST DANGEROUS SPY: WE MUST FIND HER

AND DESTROY HER! Her network in Lyon was exposed and openly hunted. Many of her most loyal allies were arrested, tortured, and sent to Nazi concentration camps. Each time, the Germans tortured them and demanded to know where "that dangerous terrorist woman" was hiding.[29]

On January 19, 1943, Virginia flew from Spain to London, where she was received as a hero. She took the time to get Cuthbert fixed and debrief SOE headquarters. But as the news of her friends' arrests reached her, she grew sick to her stomach and told headquarters she wanted to return to the field.[30]

The answer from SOE was firm: no.[31]

But Virginia was not one to take no for an answer. She was a problem solver. Cuthbert had forced her to solve all kinds of problems over the years. What was one more? While the SOE had her chained to a boring desk job in London, she began to make inquiries. She turned to an old friend who was stationed in England working for the Office of Strategic Services (OSS)—the United States' fledgling intelligence unit and the precursor to the CIA. OSS was desperate for recruits—just like the Brits had been a few years ago—so desperate that OSS was willing to accept a one-legged woman, albeit with more experience in her pinky than most of the men combined in the field.[32]

It took more than a year for her plan to come together, and not a moment too soon. The Allied forces were getting ready to invade Europe, and they needed the Resistance members to be in fighting form. There are no do-overs in war. They only had one shot to get it right.

In March 1944, an old lady walked along the beaches of northern France, struggling against the wind. If you looked very closely and you knew what you were looking for, you might have seen the traces of a familiar face. But "Diane" had gone to considerable lengths to disguise herself as an elderly French peasant. She dyed her hair, painted elaborate wrinkles on her face, filed down her smooth American teeth, and practiced a new gait. Virginia Hall hadn't stepped foot in France in sixteen months. Now, she was back under the auspices of the OSS. She was ready to finish what she'd started.[33]

Over the next three months, Virginia rebuilt Resistance units in central France, trained small groups in the art of guerilla warfare, and ferried arms and explosives to trustworthy agents. The plan was simple. The D-day invasion was imminent. As soon as Allied forces touched down in Normandy, Resistance members were supposed to do whatever they could to sabotage the German military.[34] When June 6, 1944, arrived, the Resistance—at Virginia's direction—

sprang into action. They destroyed railways, planted roadblocks, demolished bridges, cut telephone wires, damaged and blew up German vehicles, and lobbed direct attacks against German soldiers.[35]

The French response was overwhelming. Thousands of French citizens wanted to play even a small part in defeating the Nazis. It was Virginia's role to vet them, organize them, direct them, and arm them. Those who worked with her on the ground marveled at her sense of purpose and resoluteness in the heat of battle. She moved constantly to avoid detection; she was everywhere and nowhere at the same time. She was a force to be reckoned with.[36]

In late August, Virginia and her Resistance army fended off a German convoy for several days. On August 22, 1944, the Germans surrendered. They had freed their region in south-central France. On August 24, Allied forces reached Paris, and thanks to Virginia's reconnaissance in the early months of the year, they were able to set the French capital free.[37]

Over her spectacular career, Virginia went by many names. Marie. Isabelle. Philomène. Diane. La Madone. The Limping Lady. These names reflected the reality of her life. She was always hiding a part of herself. That changed in the last spurts of the war, when she fell in love with, and ultimately married, one of her OSS boys, Paul

Gaston Goillot. With Paul, she could finally drop the mask and be herself.[38]

It is hard to imagine the grueling life Virginia led during her three years in France. Always on edge. Always looking over her shoulder. Always listening for the slightest sound in the dead of night. Always escaping by the skin of her teeth. Always doubting. Never being at peace. It was a terrifying existence compounded by extreme weather, lack of resources, and exhaustion, not to mention good old Cuthbert, which remained a poor excuse for a leg. And still Virginia describes those years as the greatest freedom she experienced in her life. She felt purposeful and useful. She felt alive.

Virginia was constantly rejected, and yet she never stopped serving. She insisted on jumping back into the lion's den time and again. When President Harry Truman wanted to award her the Distinguished Service Cross—the army's second-highest military honor—she initially resisted. As an undercover agent, she viewed public honors as unnecessary and careless. For her, serving was a way of life, a duty. When the war ended, she returned to America and joined the newly founded CIA, becoming "the first woman operations officer in the entire covert action arm of the CIA," though she continued to butt heads with the unimaginative bureaucrats in Washington.[39] Only when she died in 1982 did historians begin to dig into everything she had accomplished and start to tell her story.

Service can mean a lot of different things and take many different shapes. Virginia's story is filled with real people who exemplified service in their own way. The French Resistance was a web of thousands of people working in concert. She escaped capture—and certain torture—often thanks to the kindness and integrity of strangers.

Throughout my life, I have met many people who find the courage to serve in their own way. I am blessed to have a wonderful husband who serves in the National Guard. I have also met teachers, mothers and fathers, doctors, and volunteers who change people's lives every day without ever stepping onto the battlefield. Most of them don't ever receive recognition for their service. Most don't seek it.

Service isn't always flashy or thrilling. Sometimes, it is small and intangible. Sometimes, you might not even realize how much you're helping and giving back. It doesn't matter. If your heart is in the right place, if you know what you believe, if you put other people first, then you're on the right track.

9

I stood at the starting line waiting for the horn to go off. I was nervous. I had trained for this moment, but there are always the voices in your head that say, "Maybe this wasn't a good idea. Maybe you will fail." Then, I heard the dense sound fill the South Carolina air, and I was off. One foot in front of the other, music blasting in my ears. There were no doubts, no fears. There was just running.

This wasn't the Olympics—not by a long shot. It was my first race as an amateur runner and my first half marathon. I took up running after I left the United Nations because I needed a new challenge. I have always needed to push myself to try new—and scary—things. When I ran for the state legislature, when I ran for governor, when I came to the United Nations, I always made sure I never got too comfortable. That's why I signed up to run a half marathon—because I had always thought I couldn't be a runner.

That's normal. New experiences, new jobs, even new hobbies can push you past your comfort zone. But, never forget, fear holds us back and keeps us from realizing our dreams. If you refuse to give in to fear, you can accomplish anything.

Growing up in our small town of Bamberg,

South Carolina, I often wondered why I didn't see anyone who looked like me in a position of authority. I told my parents, "One day, I'm going to be the mayor of Bamberg!" My parents laughed and said I could do anything if I put my mind to it. And the crazy thing is, I believed them.

I had a good life, but there were challenging moments. Whether it was being the only female supervisor on an all-male corporate team or running for office in the state with the fewest female elected officials, I never seemed to fit the mold. I learned something important: If you don't fit the mold, break the mold. Our job won't be done until we know our daughters won't have any molds left to break.

In the corporate world, at one of my first executive meetings, I was asked to get the CEO a cup of coffee. I had my assistant get it for him instead. They didn't ask me to get coffee again. When I ran for the statehouse, people told me I was too young and had small children to look after. It was actually a woman who told me I wasn't ready for the statehouse and I should start at the school board level. That one hurt.

Then, I ran for governor, and no woman or minority had ever held the office, so people assumed I couldn't win. Finally, when I got to the United Nations, I thought the challenges would be over. But sure enough, I was told by my counterparts that I was too bold and should back off a bit. Well, clearly, I didn't listen to that advice either.

I say all of this to remind you not to let anyone define what you can do. Only you can do that. Don't let others—or yourself—limit what you are capable of. There were never any lines to the women's bathroom in any of the jobs or positions I have held. I always wished there were. But I felt my job was to change that in my own small way. If I gave up, then the next woman after me might give up, too. And we would never change anything.

Wilma Rudolph faced some very big obstacles. She had a lot of smart experts telling her she would never walk again. She was just five years old—what did she know? Except she knew deep in her heart what she could accomplish if she didn't let fear get in the way. She pushed through the fear, or rather, she ran through it, and came out the other side stronger and prouder.

When I crossed the finish line of my half marathon, I knew that same feeling. I was exhausted, but I felt strong. I had done something that scared me, something I thought I couldn't do. I put in the miles and trained day after day, week after week, and then I proved myself wrong. It was worth it.

Wilma Rudolph

Never Give Up

My doctor told me I would never walk again. My mother told me I would. I believed my mother.[1]

—WILMA RUDOLPH

In every situation, go in knowing that you deserve to be in the room and prove it.

—NIKKI HALEY

Wilma Rudolph was just twenty years old, staring down the biggest moment of her young life. She was thousands of miles and an ocean away from home. The crowd at the Stadio Olimpico track was electric. But no one was looking at her. Nobody expected anything from her. She knew better. She knew how hard it had been to get to this point. She knew the hours of therapy it took to even dream of walking—let alone running in the Olympic Games. She knew the humiliation and anguish she endured during her childhood, always feeling like she was broken, like she wasn't good enough. She knew she wouldn't be the fastest out of the blocks—

she was never the best starter—but it would only take seconds for her legs to fly across the earth. She knew what she could do in the span of just eleven seconds.

She could win.

Not once. Not twice. But three times. She brought three gold medals home from Rome in 1960—the first American woman to do so. She captured the world's imagination and reminded America that its best days were still ahead. She changed women's sports and continues to serve as an inspiration to millions of girls who refuse to give up on their dreams.

Wilma Rudolph's story reads like a fairy tale, except there were no fairy godmothers and no magic spells. Everything she did to overcome the obstacles in her life came from her—her tenacity, her training, her disappointment after defeat, and her refusal to give up. It is a remarkable story about a remarkable young woman.

Born on June 23, 1940, in Clarksville, Tennessee, Wilma's early arrival was a sign of the struggles to come. She was born two months premature and weighed just four and a half pounds. She was the twentieth of her father's twenty-two children, and there was plenty of love to go around but not much else. She grew up in poverty in a wood-frame house with no electricity and no indoor bathrooms.[2]

Sickness came early and often. Scarlet fever.

Double pneumonia. Measles. Mumps. Whooping cough. Some of those illnesses almost killed her. She also had polio—a virus that had already claimed thousands of young lives and disabled many more. The lifesaving polio vaccine wouldn't be discovered for another ten years, and Wilma would become another polio statistic. By the time she was five, polio left her left leg twisted and weak.[3]

She was five years old when she was given a steel brace to straighten her leg and help her regain mobility. The brace went from the top of her knee down to her shoe, and she always had to wear the same ugly brown shoe. She hated it. To Wilma, the brace was a prison and a constant reminder that she was different. It weighed on her—physically and emotionally.[4]

The brace and home exercises prescribed by the local doctor weren't working. Maybe the doctors were right. Maybe she would never walk again. But Wilma's mother didn't give up. Twice a week (later it would be once a week), Wilma and her mother or an aunt boarded the bus for Meharry Hospital in Nashville, fifty miles away. Wilma was only six years old.[5]

The doctors offered no guarantees, but they offered hope. They put Wilma on an exhausting regimen of heat and water therapy and therapeutic massages. Her mother and siblings took turns massaging her leg four times a day. Every week, after the long trip home, Wilma would inspect her leg to see if it looked any better.[6]

Slowly, Wilma claimed one small victory after another. It wasn't long before she could hop on one leg. At age eight, she could walk with a steel leg brace.[7] At age nine, she took off her brace and walked into her family's church, to the surprise of her entire community. The parish cheered, and Wilma drew strength from that moment—"one of the most important moments" in her life. She was finally showing everyone that she was more than a sick kid. At ten, she stopped her treatments in Nashville, and at twelve, she could walk without any braces, crutches, or orthopedic shoes. Her mother packaged up the brace and sent it back to the hospital. She was "free at last."[8]

Those years were hard. Walking with the brace meant she could finally go to school, but she couldn't play with the other kids, and they called her names like "cripple."[9] "I remember the kids always saying, 'I don't want to play with her. We don't want her on our team,'" she said. Her competitive spirit was lit and stoked during those early years of rejection. While others may have seen it as a reason not to try, it was Wilma's fuel. "And all my young life I would say, 'One day I'm going to be somebody very special. And I'm not going to forget those kids.'"[10]

When Wilma finally shed the brace, therapy, and special shoes, she felt like she got a new lease on life. The normalcy that she craved was finally within grasp. "I went from being a sickly kid the other kids teased to a normal person accepted by my peer group, and that was the most important thing that could have happened to me at that point in my life. I needed to belong, and I finally did."[11]

As she prepared to enter junior high school, Wilma wanted to prove that she could do more than walk. No one expected her to be an athlete of any kind. But she had already proven the doctors wrong. Why not prove everyone else wrong, too? She began playing basketball with her brothers, and it turned out she was pretty good. Playing basketball was the first indication of Wilma's natural athleticism and her commitment to perfection. Although she sat on the bench for the entirety of seventh and eighth grade, she practiced constantly. She studied the game and ran drills. She was determined to earn her spot on the court. When she did, she also earned something else—a nickname that would stay with her throughout her life. Her coach called her "Skeeter" because she was fast like a mosquito and buzzed all around.[12]

The more she practiced, the more aware she became that girls playing sports was not exactly accepted. People said discouraging things like "playing sports will give you muscles" and "if you run around too much as a girl you'll never be able to have children." But Wilma loved playing sports and loved dressing up. She pursued her own path.[13]

In eighth grade, Wilma joined the track team, easily winning local meets. She didn't know anything about technique or training. All she knew how to do was run, and she was fast. But soon she would learn there is a lot more to running. She would also learn the importance of losing.[14]

In her sophomore year, her track team was invited to a meet at the Tuskegee Institute, where Coach Abbott was famous for producing champions and Tuskegee athletes had won the Amateur Athletic Union (AAU) championship nearly every year for the past twenty years. Wilma was unprepared for this level of competition. She lost all her races, and it hit her hard. "I was totally crushed," she said. "I can't remember ever being so totally crushed by anything." She had tasted defeat, and she didn't like it one bit; she never wanted to experience that feeling again.[15]

Wilma started running every chance she had. She faked illness to get out of class and run, until her teachers realized she looked too healthy. Every day she ran, promising herself she would "never, never give up, no matter what else happened." Slowly, she also learned that losing is part of life. "Nobody goes undefeated all the time," she wrote. "If you can pick up after a crushing defeat, and go on to win again, you are going to be a champion someday."[16]

Soon, Wilma got a break. Tennessee State University's coach Ed Temple volunteered as the referee for Wilma's high school basketball games. He spotted her talent and invited her to participate in his summer program in Nashville. Coach Temple changed Wilma's life. Wilma was a natural athlete, but she lacked the formal training and rigor necessary to turn a good athlete into a world-class champion. Coach Temple was the missing piece.[17]

Ed Temple was a committed coach—the kind who fixed the school track with his own money and drove his team to meets in his own car. He was also tough. His summer athletes sometimes ran twenty miles a day, and he expected them to give him their all.[18] Soon, Tennessee State's Tigerbelles became a force to be reckoned with in women's athletics.

In 1956, Wilma competed in the Olympic trials at Coach Temple's urging for a spot at the Melbourne games. Unlike many athletes who dream of the Olympics their whole lives, it was not something she thought about or even fully grasped. She had never heard of Melbourne, Australia, before. Of course, that didn't matter. Wilma Rudolph, the girl who wasn't supposed to walk, was going to the Olympics.[19]

In Melbourne, Wilma came in third in the

200-meter semifinals and didn't advance to the next round, but she took home a bronze medal with her teammates in the 400-meter relay. Wilma stood proudly on the medal stand, but there was a part of her that couldn't shake the disappointment of coming up short in the 200 meters. Ever since she was a little girl, Wilma had been her own toughest critic.[20] She came back to the United States certain of one thing: Next time, there would be no bronze medal. There would only be gold.[21]

Four years later, Wilma Rudolph headed to Rome in the best condition of her life. She ran so fast during the AAU national championship that her own coach wondered if the track was missing a few yards.[22] But there was little buzz about Wilma or her teammates. The American experts put their money on Australian "Golden Girl" Betty Cuthbert, who had won three golds in Melbourne four years before. They expected the Russians and the Germans to make up the rest of the medal podium. In fact, Olympic officials refused to believe Wilma's sprint times, placing her in a lower seed and forcing her to compete against faster runners in her early heats.[23]

On September 2, Wilma got ready for the finals in the 100-meter dash—the race that awarded the title of "fastest woman in the world." The mood in the stands was not optimistic. The day before, on "Black Thursday," the world watched American favorites in the men's races come up short, and the press blamed it on too much partying. One U.S. official complained, "You can't catch any Russian out dancing after ten!"[24]

Wilma seemed unfazed. She even managed to fall asleep and catch an afternoon nap before her run. She woke to Coach Temple yelling, "Time to wake up, Wilma. Time to run! Time to run!" She laced up her shoes and entered the track in her white shorts and blue-and-red shirt with the number 17 painted on the back.[25]

The gun went off. Wilma flew out of the starting blocks. Long and lanky, she made running look effortless, like she was floating across the track. She was the first to break the tape. As she slowed to a jog, those paying attention could notice a small limp, the result of a twisted ankle during practice that week. It hadn't slowed her down one bit.[26]

Her time was eleven seconds flat, the fastest time ever for a female sprinter. Now, everyone was paying attention to the lanky American. She went from being a nobody to being an international star, from being a Tennessee Tigerbelle to being the "belle of the Olympics." It wasn't just her gold-medal-winning run. Fans were drawn to her story and her kind and easygoing nature. Crowds mobbed her everywhere she went in Rome, insisting on getting a photo with *"La Gazella Nera"*—the "Black Gazelle." She became an instant inspiration to her fellow athletes and the millions of people tuned in to the Olympic Games.[27]

The 1960 Olympics in Rome were the first commercially televised Summer Games.[28] For the first time, Americans could see great athletes competing on the screen instead of just hearing or reading about them. Americans could put faces to the names filling the newspaper stories. As the saying goes, seeing is believing, and there was something special about seeing Wilma run. She had a beautiful stride. She almost always started out behind (her height made her a mediocre starter),[29] but she easily covered the distance and sped past her competitors. It was eleven seconds of pure adrenaline and old-fashioned American pride. TV made that possible. America was in love with Skeeter.

Three days later, on September 5, Wilma stepped onto the track for the 200-meter semi-finals and finals. This time, she was not an unknown athlete but a superstar. The eyes of the world were glued to her. For Wilma, this race had a special meaning. Four years earlier, she lost out on the chance to race in the preliminary heats. Since then, the 200 had become her best distance. This day was no exception. In the semifinals, she set a new Olympic record at 23.2 seconds and then clinched her second gold medal in the finals.[30] Wilma was on her way to making history.

The 400-meter relay took place three days before the closing ceremony. The four American Tigerbelles prayed together, and Wilma, the anchor, told her teammates, "Just get me that stick. Just get me that stick, and we're going to get on that stand. We're going to win that gold medal!"[31]

It's easy for spectators to forget the importance of the baton—or the stick—in the relay. All it takes is one slippery handoff and the baton drops to the ground along with the athletes' Olympic dreams. Coach Temple forced his runners to practice passing the baton seamlessly over and over again.[32] Wilma and her teammates had done it a thousand times before. But they had to do it one more time—when it mattered most.

As Lucinda Williams rounded the track, she was running so fast that Wilma almost missed the baton. Almost. She paused to make sure she had the baton in her grasp, and the sloppy handoff put Wilma behind. Of course, it didn't matter. Wilma was unstoppable. Once she started running, she could catch anyone. She won the race by five yards over the second-place finisher. The Germans never had a chance.[33]

Wilma Rudolph made history, becoming the first American woman to win three gold medals in a single Olympics. She and the rest of the team spent more than two weeks traveling across Europe meeting fans and participating in international meets. They were greeted by thousands of students on their return to Tennessee State University and honored at the Tennessee State Capitol.[34] Her hometown of Clarksville hosted a parade and a banquet in her honor and proclaimed Tuesday, October 4, Wilma Rudolph Day.[35]

Wilma Rudolph's victory came at a time when the world desperately needed a win. For athletes, she represented triumph after years of hard work. They all knew the agony of defeat and the hope of redemption. Every elite athlete deals with injuries, losses, setbacks, and the persistent, unfailing dream of a gold medal around their necks. Wilma faced more setbacks than most, and now she had not one but three gold medals to show for her efforts.

For female athletes in particular, Wilma's victory marked the beginning of a new era when the world began to take them seriously. Change didn't happen overnight, but as Coach Temple said, "For every woman athlete who came after, she was the person who opened the door."[36] America would end up being a dominant force in women's track and field, with famous icons like Florence Griffith Joyner, Jackie Joyner-Kersee, Gail Devers, Mary Decker, and Allyson Felix. These women grew up with Wilma Rudolph as an inspiration. When Wilma was growing up, she didn't have anyone to look up to.

For America, Wilma's story punctured the tension of the Cold War and gave the free world an unlikely champion. By the time the Rome Olympics kicked off in 1960, U.S.–Soviet hostilities had reached new heights. Only a few months before, an American reconnaissance plane was shot down over Soviet airspace and pilot Francis Gary Powers was arrested by Soviet officials.[37] On August 17, just a few days before the Rome Olympics began, Russia initiated a sham trial of Powers on espionage charges.[38]

The power struggle between the United States and the Soviet Union permeated the games. American athletes were determined not just to win but to beat the Communists. Conversely, the Soviet Union told its athletes that winning would show the world the power and glory of Communism.[39]

Along came Wilma Rudolph and stomped all over the Russians and the rest of the world on the Stadio Olimpico track. She wasn't just a track star. She was an American hero who beat unbeatable odds.

As the world grew increasingly dangerous, Wilma was a symbol of hope. With her generous smile and galloping stride, she reminded Americans that anything is possible, especially if you refuse to give up.

It is a timeless lesson.

Take it to heart.

We all have obstacles to overcome. We all have painful moments and dashed dreams. On your darkest days, remember Wilma. Remember your fate is not sealed in stone. Today's hardships are not the end of your story but the beginning. Tomorrow's bad news does not define you. Your future is wide open with possibilities, so long as you dive in headfirst and hold nothing back.

10

The word feminism is complicated, but it doesn't have to be. It should mean simply that women are granted the same legal rights and protections under the law as men have—not more, not less. It should mean that women can take their own paths in life just as much as men do. If they want to teach, let them teach. If they want to run for political office, let them run. If they want to focus on raising children, let them do that. Above all, we should view girls and women as individuals, each with her own set of talents, dreams, and life plans.

Somewhere along the way, feminism got twisted. It is now used as a political club to browbeat people into sticking to a preapproved script. Women (and men) are told what to believe, how to vote, what careers to choose—all in the name of so-called feminism. This hypocrisy is lost on liberals. Women fought for so long to have the freedom to make their own decisions, only to be boxed in by a woke mob telling them how to live and think.

No, thank you. It's time for us to reclaim feminism.

Growing up, I certainly met my share of people who thought I should choose a different path because of my gender. Our country had come a long way in giving women equal rights, but some people still needed forceful nudges in the right direction. I could have been angry. I could have yelled or quit. But I found the best way forward was to show people they were wrong and not let people's mistakes define me or them.

When some thought I couldn't win, I changed their minds by working harder than my opponents. When legislators thought I couldn't get bills passed, we proved them wrong by going to the people and forcing the legislature to do the right thing. I could have thrown a tantrum and played the victim, but what would that have accomplished?

It sometimes seems like you can't be a feminist today if you aren't angry at someone or railing against something. Some strains of radical feminism are outwardly anti-men. When we don't like what a man does or says, it is painted as "sexist" or "mansplaining" instead of dealing with the substance and the facts.

Feminism today is filled with tropes about what men should do to empower women. They should interrupt less, go out of their way to ask women what they think, rephrase questions to be more inclusive. That is a vast overreach and is often unfair to men. I prefer to focus on how we can teach young girls and women to empower themselves, to speak their minds, and to follow their own dreams no matter what anyone else says. Victimhood should never be the answer. Working hard and proving you deserve to be in the room is what will improve your life and the lives of women who come after you.

Men and women are different in some ways. It's biology. There's no denying that, and we shouldn't pretend otherwise. Some of those differences matter. Most of them don't. It's unfortunate, for example, that when women run for public office, the media often comments on their clothes, their hairstyles, and their weight far more so than they do about male candidates. It would be better for everyone if they ignored that superficial stuff. But guess what? Life isn't always fair. Thankfully, we live in a time in which far more options are available to women. And when they're not, we need to make them available.

Today, no one questions whether women can fly airplanes as well as men. That was not always the case. More than anyone else, a woman named Amelia Earhart broke that barrier. Her story is about a lot more than flying.

The world is fascinated with Amelia Earhart, in part because she disappeared trying to break another record—the longest flight around the world. But long before she disappeared, she was admired because of her accomplishments and her pursuit of greatness. When she took on the male-dominated organizations that shut female fliers out, she didn't try to tear down the great male pilots of her time. She explained matter-of-factly why the prevailing assumptions about women were wrong, and then she changed people's minds by showing them she could fly just as well as men.

Amelia Earhart was a feminist, but she was also an individualist. She flew airplanes because she loved the freedom of flight. She felt most alive when she was thousands of feet above the ground, plunging through the clouds. She didn't do it because she was trying to make a point or teach men a lesson. It was who she was, and she didn't see any reason why she had to change or adapt. Instead, she believed—correctly—that the world should adapt to make room for women like her.

When Amelia Earhart and her cohorts founded the Ninety-Nines—an all-female flying club— the members came in all shapes and sizes. There were mothers, teachers, writers, mechanics, journalists, and actresses. They were fearless individuals who shared a passion for flying. That is what made them great.

When I look at conservative leadership in this country, I see women from all kinds of backgrounds running for (and winning) office. There are young moms and empty nesters. There are doctors, veterans, pilots, journalists, farmers, business owners, and so many others. They are individuals with their own sets of beliefs and principles seeking to play a role in making our country better.

That's exactly the way it should be.

Amelia Earhart

If You're Going to Do Something, Do It Well

Never do things others can do and will do, if there are things others cannot do or will not do.[1]

—AMELIA EARHART

Whatever you do, be great at it, and make sure people remember you for it.

—NIKKI HALEY

In the early days of aviation, flying was a magical venture—and a dangerous one. The fact that Amelia Earhart disappeared in flight never to be found again is one of the most normal parts of her story. Planes were unreliable, and pilots pushed the limits of science and gravity. Everyone wanted to be the first at something. The first to cross the Atlantic. The first to fly coast-to-coast from east to west. The first to fly solo. The first to fly around the world. The first to fly faster, higher, longer.[2] The sad truth is many pilots didn't survive to report on their attempts.

After Charles Lindbergh became the first person to fly solo across the Atlantic Ocean in

1927, people lined up to follow in his footsteps. Fifty-five people and eighteen planes tried in the subsequent twelve months. Eight pilots succeeded. Fourteen died. The rest failed.[3]

When Amelia Earhart disappeared into the clouds over Howland Island in 1937, her life story was plunged into mystery. The question "What happened to Amelia Earhart?" became the defining feature of her nearly forty years. It is the wrong question. The more important question is: What made Amelia Earhart great? What makes her legacy so enduring?

To be sure, she was talented. She was smart, charming, and unassuming. She was also fearless. She was passionate about flying and refused to be anyone other than herself. She used that passion to set a slew of aeronautical records, to support other female aviators, and to demand the respect women like her deserved.

Amelia took up flying in 1920 and set her first record in 1922.[4] World fame, however, happened by accident. It was what she did with that fame that sets her apart.

In 1928, wealthy publisher and publicist George P. Putnam and his colleague were looking for the "right sort of girl." She had to be attractive, compelling, and of "good breeding," and it would be nice if she could fly a plane, though that was not a necessity.[5] Someone told them, "Call

Denison House and ask for Amelia Earhart." That's exactly what they did.[6]

A wealthy female aviator was supposed to attempt a cross-Atlantic trip, making her the first woman to fly across the Atlantic, but the woman backed out at the last minute. The trip's backers needed a replacement. Would Amelia be interested?[7]

She signed up to be the commander of a $60,000 tri-motored seaplane named the *Friendship*. She would not physically fly the plane, nor would she earn any compensation for her time and effort. In contrast, the pilot, Bill Stultz, and the mechanic, Lou Gordon, would be rewarded generously. After all, this was 1928, and according to Amelia, "Flying is still a man's game."[8]

On June 3, Earhart, Stultz, and Gordon woke at 3:30 a.m. It took the team five tries to achieve takeoff—making it only after they dumped gas, gear, and the backup pilot. As soon as they lifted off, the cabin door opened and Gordon and Earhart almost fell out. They rigged the door shut with a piece of string. When they finally landed in Trepassey, Newfoundland, for an overnight refueling stop, they met weather trouble. Their one-night stay turned into two weeks.[9]

June 13 was no better than any of the other days. Two storms headed their way, but Amelia was tired of waiting and tired of eating canned rabbit. "We're going today," she informed her hungover pilot. Stultz protested, certain they were flying into their graves, but Amelia didn't take no for an answer.[10]

The flight to Ireland was not glamorous. Amelia didn't have a seat, and the cushions she was supposed to sit on were dumped in their efforts to lighten the plane's load. It was cold, sometimes freezing. And she wasn't flying. Her only job was to keep a log on the flight and record everything she saw. But as the hours passed, they didn't see the most important thing—land. They were running out of gas and had no idea where they were.[11]

Finally, like an oasis appearing in the fog, they spied a stretch of land. It wasn't Ireland, but it didn't matter. Wales was good enough. They had done it! They had flown across the Atlantic and touched down on European soil. Stultz landed the plane in the water, and they floated quietly to the shore. Soon, there would be no more quiet.[12]

Amelia became an instant celebrity. She was the first woman to fly across the Atlantic—even if she didn't do any flying. She was inundated with reporters, cameras, and probing questions about her life. There was a homecoming parade and hundreds of thousands of people thronging the streets of Boston to catch a glimpse of the famous Amelia Earhart. She was, according to the newspaper articles, "the best-known girl in America."[13]

Her life was forever changed. But her newfound celebrity status rubbed her the wrong way. By her account, she hadn't done much of anything except sit on a plane. "I was just baggage," she said. "Like a sack of potatoes."[14] Amelia wasn't interested in fame for fame's sake. She wanted to accomplish something. She wanted to fly.

She would soon have her chance thanks to a man named Cliff Henderson. Henderson was a salesman and showman, and he loved the sport of flying. In the late 1920s, he had staged a number of flying derbies, attracting national attention and record-breaking crowds. He was approached with the idea of organizing an all-female derby from Los Angeles to Cleveland—a two-thousand-mile trip—and he jumped at the idea.[15]

There was one problem. The race organizers and funders were all men, and they doubted women had the stamina to handle such a long trip. They proposed a shorter derby. That was insulting enough. Then came the slap in the face: Each woman had to fly with a man.[16]

Amelia and her fellow aviators were furious and threatened Henderson with a boycott. "If we can't fly the race and navigate our own course through the Rockies, I, for one, won't enter," Amelia declared. "How is a fellow going to earn his spurs without at least trying to ride?"[17]

A compromise was reached. The women could fly from California on their own, but they had to be serious pilots with hours of training under their belts. They also had to make overnight stops for a total of fifteen stops along the way. The women agreed.[18]

In September 1929, the stage was set for the "greatest show on earth," according to Henderson. There was a lot at stake for the women. For starters, staying alive was not a guarantee. And winning the prize money was a big perk for many of the women, who had to scrape together funds to keep their flying careers alive. But the elite fliers recognized this was not just about winning. With the eyes of the country on them, this was about showing the world they could fly just as long, just as hard, and just as fast. The men "seem to have visions of us smashing up all over the countryside," Earhart said. "So the thing for us to do is to prove their fears have been foolish." As the aviators boarded their planes and prepared for the next two thousand-plus miles, they knew what they needed to do. They needed to be better than good. They needed to be great.[19]

As the race began, the official name of the derby—the National Women's Air Derby— was soon replaced with nicknames. They were not intended as compliments. The Powder Puff Derby. The She Derby. The Cosmetic Caravan. Will Rogers wrote in his nationally syndicated column, "They are aviators, but they are still women."[20]

Nineteen fliers left Santa Monica on August 18, 1929. Sixteen finishers landed in Cleveland. Louise Thaden came in first, Gladys O'Donnell in second, and Earhart in third. One of the pilots died.[21]

Some people blamed the women for the tragedy. "Women are lacking in certain qualities that men possess," Oklahoma businessman Erle Halliburton said. "Handling details essential to safe flying is one of the qualifications women have not mastered successfully." Columnist Arthur Brisbane thought it was a waste for women to fly and risk their lives when they could be doing more important things, like being mothers. "Such races should be confined to men," he opined.[22] Charles Lindbergh, the "Columbus of the Air," would not give the women the time of day. A constant presence in the press, Lindbergh refused to comment on the all-female derby.[23]

It's worth noting—and the women did—that male fliers faced similar if not worse mishaps during previous derbies. Flying in 1929 was a dirty, brutal, and deadly venture. In Henderson's all-male transcontinental derby from Los Angeles to New York, only one out of nine planes touched ground in the Big Apple. Storms, mechanical issues, crash landings, hard-to-read maps—it was all par for the course.[24]

The women who made it to Cleveland met up after the celebrations. Earhart had long wanted to form an alliance of sorts, mentioning her idea for a female flying club to Ruth Nichols in 1927. Now, the women had their motivation.[25]

Twenty-six women, including five of the Powder Puff fliers, met that year at a hangar on Long Island. Their goal wasn't to stand against the men but to stand up for themselves and each other. It was about women having each other's backs. They sent invitations to 117 women to join their new club. Earhart suggested that they wait to see how many women accepted to decide on a name. That's how they became known as the Ninety-Nines. Elected as the group's first president in 1931, Amelia hoped the Ninety-Nines would help women become not just great fliers—but also "true individuals."[26]

Was that too much to ask?

For some, it was. In 1930, Cliff Henderson planned a repeat of his widely successful Powder Puff Derby. But Earhart, Thaden, Nichols, and others were incensed by the unfair rules and double standards. Women weren't allowed to compete against men and were required to fly with an escort of a doctor and two U.S. Army planes. New rules also limited the power of their engines. The reason for these absurd restrictions? According to the officials, "Without power restrictions, the prettiest flier would probably get the biggest plane of the best manufacturer, and if her luck and her flying skills held out she would probably reach Chicago first." The Ninety-Nines refused to participate.[27]

Amelia still felt like she had something to prove. In the spring of 1932, she plotted her "grudge flight." It annoyed her that she was famous for flying as a passenger. It was time for her to show the world that she could fly across the Atlantic on her own.[28]

On May 20, her red Lockheed departed Canada for Europe—exactly five years after Charles Lindbergh had left New York for Paris. Amelia, too, hoped to make it to Paris, but fate had other plans. She flew calmly for several hours until one thing after another went wrong. A broken altimeter meant she had no idea how high or low she was flying. An unexpected storm caused ice to gather on her wings. And then there was the leaking fuel and cracked exhaust manifold. She wasn't going to reach Paris. She just hoped she could reach land—somewhere.[29]

She found somewhere—a farmer's field near Londonderry, Northern Ireland, to be exact. Amelia Earhart became the fourteenth person to fly east across the Atlantic and the first woman. She was only the second person to do it solo— after Charles Lindbergh.[30] She had finally proven to herself and the world that she belonged in the pantheon of great fliers.

The door truly seemed to open in September 1933, when Cliff Henderson hosted another derby and invited men *and* women to compete side by side in a speed race. Earhart was sidelined with engine trouble, but up-and-comer Florence Klingensmith jumped at the opportunity, choosing the controversial Gee Bee plane—a new model built for speed that had already been in several high-profile fatal accidents. Klingensmith's name was soon added to the tragic list.[31]

Two other Gee Bee planes had crashed in the past three days,[32] but that didn't stop the coroner's investigators from insisting on a new explanation. They turned to a U.S. Department of Commerce rule that said no woman is allowed to fly "within a period extending from 3 days prior, to 3 days after, the menstrual period." Since Klingensmith was never inspected before she flew, it was entirely possible that she was in a "weakened condition" due to her period.[33]

The men who had just opened the door to women fliers now slammed the door shut. Cliff Henderson had a change of heart. "Miss Florence Klingensmith's fatal crash in Chicago in 1933, in a closed-course race, only proved what I already knew," he said. He would no longer allow women to compete.[34]

Amelia used her celebrity status and busy lecture schedule to fight for equality in the air and on the ground. A tomboy growing up, it irked her that girls were pushed into "girl" activities. "As a matter of fact, I know a great many boys who should be making pies—and a great many girls who would be better off in manual training," she told her audience at Barnard College. "There is no reason why a woman can't hold any position in aviation providing she can overcome prejudices and show ability."[35]

In her autobiography, she criticized society's tendency to put children in girl and boy boxes instead of seeing them as individuals. The obvious result was that most girls were never given the opportunity to learn the mechanical subjects and skills they would need later to excel at flying. It's not that women were incapable of flying. It's that they were never given a chance to succeed. "Too often little attention is paid to the individual talent. Instead, education goes on dividing people according to their sex, and putting them in little feminine or masculine pigeonholes."[36]

It wasn't just about flying. Amelia wanted to make it acceptable for women to pursue whatever career they wanted. She knew society was not going to roll over and let women in. They were going to have to fight for every inch. She wanted to use her position as a role model to show them how.[37]

In 1936, Earhart took a job at Purdue University in northwestern Indiana as a consultant and professor in the university's new department, the Center for the Study of Careers of Women.[38] Her main job was to inspire Purdue's young women and advise the university on how to broaden academic and educational opportunities for its female students. Her "outspoken" ideas were not widely accepted by the predominantly male campus. A men's group complained. Their gripe? "It's hard enough to get the girls to marry us as it is."[39]

Meanwhile, the Ninety-Nines continued to harass Henderson and anyone else standing in their way. In the summer of 1934, they criticized Henderson in an editorial titled "Cliff Henderson Turns Back the Clock." They pointed out that male fliers died in crashes all the time. It's just that no one paid attention.[40] As Amelia wrote in her book, "A fatal accident to a woman pilot is not a greater disaster than one to a man of equal worth. Feminine flyers have never subscribed to the supersentimental valuation placed upon their necks."[41]

Shut out from the derbies, Amelia had been busy. In January 1935, she became the first person to fly solo from Hawaii to California—a feat that had already claimed ten pilots' lives. In the spring of that year, she became the first person to fly from Los Angeles to Mexico City and then Mexico City to Newark.[42]

That year, Henderson finally relented, allowing women to rejoin the derbies *and* compete against men. Public opinion was slowly shifting, in no small part thanks to accomplished fliers like Amelia and her friends who were setting new records.[43]

In 1935, two women-led teams competed for the Bendix Trophy. In 1936, it was three, and Amelia's old friend Louise Thaden, with copilot Blanche Noyes, came in first. Laura Ingalls came in second. Every major publication reported on the women's victories.[44]

Amelia heralded these victories as proof that women were finally proving their mettle and would soon have full equality in the air. "If a woman wishes to enter important competitions, the question will be, 'Is she a good enough flier?' instead of primarily a matter of whether she wears skirts or trousers." Two years later, Jacquelin Cochran won the Bendix, shaving seven hours off Thaden's time.[45]

While flying was a solo sport, Amelia always understood that it was a collective effort for female aviators. That's why she started the Ninety-Nines. She believed as more women joined the aviation industry, the barriers would fall from the sheer weight of their insistence. Yes, flying was an individual venture, but knocking down barriers was a team sport.[46]

In 1937, Earhart had her eyes set on a new mission and a new record: the longest flight around the world.[47] We know how this story ends. On July 2, Earhart and her navigator were headed to Howland Island over the South Pacific. At 8:44 a.m., Earhart made communication for the last time. Her voice was panicked. She knew they were in trouble. They never arrived on Howland Island. On July 18, the U.S. government stopped searching for her.[48]

The mystery and tragedy of Amelia's last flight consumed her legacy, but her struggles and accomplishments are so much bigger than the conspiracy theories that cropped up after her disappearance. Amelia Earhart loved flying and having a career at a time when most women didn't do either. She wanted other women with similar dreams to have the same opportunity to make those dreams come true. She also believed that aviation would become the next big thing, and women would be an important part of that progress if they were given the chance. She was right.

Amelia Earhart was the most famous female pilot in the world, but she never saw herself as more important than her fellow trailblazers. When one of her fellow Ninety-Nines succeeded, it contributed to all their success. She was surrounded by doubters, but she fought back by refusing to doubt herself, by encouraging other women to do the same, and by showing the world what she was capable of, knowing that eventually her record-breaking accomplishments would convert the critics.

That is why she was so beloved and admired, why the crowds gathered to witness her record-breaking landings. She left a legacy that still inspires women today. A legacy to pursue greatness without losing oneself in the process. A legacy to share that greatness with others and pave the path for future adventurers. A legacy to embrace life and live it to the fullest, knowing that it could disappear in an instant in one final smashup.

There continues to be endless mystery about how Amelia Earhart's life ended, but there is little mystery as to how her life was lived. It was lived fearlessly, generously, and without reservation.

Sometimes it seems like we live in a zero-sum game, where one person's success detracts from another person's. Or we think we can only be successful by trampling on other people on our way to the top. Or that being great demands a certain isolation or mean streak. That's simply not true. We are so much stronger when we join together with others. We are so much better off when we use our personal success to help others succeed.

Amelia Earhart taught us that you can be fiercely competitive and true to yourself without sacrificing other people in the process. That giving back to others is part of the path to greatness. Amelia understood what it meant to put a ladder down for other women, saving them from the steps of hardship she encountered.

Amelia Earhart would have been a great aviator no matter what she did outside of the airplane. She was a great person and leader because of everything she did to help other women. She understood one woman's success was all women's success. We should learn from her legacy.

Conclusion

When I was first approached about writing this book, I was hesitant. I am a huge fan of women. I have always believed women are amazing at everything we do. We prioritize. We balance. We get things done. So why was I hesitant? Because I have always believed that women are misunderstood and often stereotyped.

Many think women are too emotional. Some think we are too ambitious. Some are convinced we are defined by one issue: whether we are pro-life or pro-choice.

That's unfortunate. I feel a kinship and sister-hood with women regardless of party. I often send supportive notes to women who have excelled in their field regardless of their political affiliation. Many have asked why I do that and waste my time. My answer: we are more than the issues the media divides us on. Growing up, I was always aware of how the media, the establishment on both sides, and academia divide women. You don't see the same bias with men.

When I focused on the profiles in this book, I didn't research if the women were Republican or Democrat. I didn't know which president they voted for. What I know is they inspired me. They inspired me because they were above the noise.

They each had one life and were determined to make the most of it. How amazing is that? They knew they were meant for great things, and they chased them until they fulfilled their purpose.

I am increasingly trying to make the most of my life and fulfill my purpose. And it's okay if you don't know your purpose yet. Just never stop searching and trying to find it. Every day you wake up, you have a choice. Either you push through the fear to find greatness or you sit on the sidelines, avoid challenges, and settle for comfort.

One of the most important things we can do in life is push through the fear. When you do that, you live life the way God intended. The amazing women highlighted in this book all pushed through the fear. They knew they were called for a higher purpose. They faced challenges head-on. They were often ridiculed and isolated. But they showed us that challenges can be overcome and are worth the fight.

I hope this book shows you that you are meant for great things whether you are fifteen, twenty-five, forty, or seventy. Women are amazingly strong. We know how to make the world a better place. We love our country, and we love the lives we are blessed to live.

I hope you will take the time to share this book with women you know, regardless of age, political party, religion, race, or ideology. Share it with them out of love. Let them know we are better because of these women, and many others.

Women face enough challenges. Let this book not be one of them. My prayer is that this book is one of bonding. A book that reminds women that there is nothing they can't do. This is a call to arms to let every woman know that you are needed to lead and heal our country. We are a sisterhood in strength. We are fighters who won't be derailed or silenced.

Let us be the leaders who love our families, love our communities, and love our country. We can remind our country what it means to be patriotic, to love thy neighbor, to focus on solutions and not arguments, to raise the next generation to be even better.

If we want to return to a strong, patriotic, loving America focused on lifting up everyone, women will lead the way because we know—as Margaret Thatcher famously said—how to get something done.

We have our work cut out for us. But we got this. Let the profiles in this book serve as our motivation, inspiration, and constant reminder. We are stronger than any label people give us. Our country is worth fighting for, and women will be the ones who save her.

Acknowledgments

This is difficult because there are so many people in my life who influenced me whether they realized it or not.

To my mom and dad, thank you for being amazing examples of strength, perseverance, courage, and love. I will never truly comprehend the challenges you faced in your life coming from India to America. I am in awe of the love you had for your children and the commitment you both shared in making sure that we all had a better life. You understood the importance of raising strong girls. I might have taken it to a new level, but I will forever be thankful you encouraged it and never held me back. God smiled when he gave me both of you as parents.

Thank you Michael, Rena, and Nalin. I'm not sure you will ever understand the love I have for you and more importantly my desire to make you proud. Everything I have accomplished in my life or will accomplish in the future is fueled by your love and support. Our life has been an adventure, but I am blessed to live it with you. Thank you for loving me through this adventurous life of ours and for the strength of the bond our family shares. I am so blessed, and I thank God every day for each one of you.

To Nachama Soloveichik, I could not have asked for a better partner in this project. You are the epitome of a badass. You are crazy smart, an amazing wife and mother, a loyal friend, and someone I would want in a foxhole with me every day of the week. Thank you for seeing the importance of this project and helping me get it to the finish line. I hope you are proud. I sure am.

To Mrs. West, my second-grade teacher, thank you for the love and kindness you showed me. While you are in heaven now, I will forever be thankful for the time you took to make me feel accepted during an uncomfortable time. You will never know the impact that had on my life. The love of a teacher is never forgotten. You will always be my favorite teacher and the one who reminded me that I deserved to be in the room.

To Joan Jett, you fill my funnel on rock 'n' roll. You broke every stereotype there was, and you were criticized and isolated for it. You never gave up and in turn reminded me to never give up. Thank you for being my musical go-to when I was down, pushed aside, or rejected. Sisters in Rock Forever.

To my sisters in arms: Life is hard, and you make it look so easy. I hope this is a reminder that you are not alone. Your intelligence, love, compassion, strength, grit, and tenacity are nothing short of awesome. Buckle up. We have a country to save. God bless each and every one of you.

Notes

Chapter 1: Margaret Thatcher

1. Nikki Haley, AIPAC Policy Conference 2017: Many Voices, One Mission, Facebook, March 31, 2017, https://www.facebook.com /watch/?v=10154482079853543.
2. Charles Moore, *Margaret Thatcher: The Authorized Biography: Volume I: From Grantham to the Falklands* (New York: First Vintage Books, 2015), 331–332.
3. Ibid., 332.
4. Ibid., 332–333.
5. Buttonwood, "Britain: Back to Being the Sick Man of Europe?" *Economist*, July 19, 2017.
6. Madsen Pirie, "Edward Heath's 'Conservative' Government," Adam Smith Institute, June 19, 2019, https://www.adamsmith.org /blog/edward-heaths-conservative-govern ment.
7. Claire Berlinski, *There Is No Alternative* (New York: Basic Books, 2008), 23.
8. Moore, *Margaret Thatcher*, 196, 263.
9. Ibid., 438.
10. Alvin Shuster, "Britain's Inflation Soars to a Record 25%," *New York Times*, June 14, 1975.
11. Moore, *Margaret Thatcher*, 316.

12. Ibid., 309–311.
13. Ibid., 316.
14. Ibid., 320.
15. Ibid., 321.
16. Rob Williams, "The Ten Worst British Winters Ever," *Independent*, November 17, 2013, https://www.independent.co.uk/news/uk/home-news/the-10-worst-british-winters-ever-8945584.html.
17. Jon Gustavsson, "Lessons from the U.K.'s Winter of Discontent," *Dispatch*, October 22, 2021, https://thedispatch.com/p/lessons-from-the-uks-winter-of-discontent?s=r; Berlinski, *There Is No Alternative*, 11–12.
18. "Jim Callaghan Press Conference 1979," YouTube video, 2:40, posted by FRiB6890, December 28, 2010, https://youtu.be/dX06xqN6710.
19. " 'Crisis? What Crisis?' " BBC News, September 12, 2000, http://news.bbc.co.uk/1/hi/uk_politics/921524.stm.
20. Moore, *Margaret Thatcher*, 431.
21. "1979: Election Victory for Margaret Thatcher," BBC News, http://news.bbc.co.uk/onthisday/hi/dates/stories/may/4/newsid_2503000/2503195.stm.
22. "What Is Thatcherism?" BBC News, April 10, 2013, https://www.bbc.com/news/uk-politics-22079683.
23. Dylan Matthews, "A Look Back at Margaret

Thatcher's Economic Record," *Washington Post*, April 8, 2013.

24. Charles Moore, "The Invincible Mrs. Thatcher," *Vanity Fair*, December 2011.

25. R. W. Apple Jr., "Mrs. Thatcher Stresses Concern for Britain's Jobless," *New York Times*, October 11, 1980.

26. Moore, *Margaret Thatcher*, 97–98.

27. "Article for *Gravesend and Dartford Reporter (YOU Will Decide),*" Margaret Thatcher Foundation, https://www.margaret thatcher.org/document/100856.

28. "Speech to Conservative Party Conference ('The Lady's Not for Turning') ['The Reason Why']," Margaret Thatcher Foundation, https://www.margaretthatcher.org/document /104431.

29. Ibid.

30. Ibid.

31. "Release of MT's Private Files for 1980-(2) 'NOT for Turning,'" Margaret Thatcher Foundation, https://www.margaretthatcher .org/archive/1980cac2.

32. Steven Rattner, "Mrs. Thatcher Firm on Her Austerity Policies," *New York Times,* October 10, 1982.

33. Richard Seymour, "A Short History of Privatisation in the UK: 1979–2012," *Guardian*, March 29, 2012.

34. Steven Rattner, "British Government Seeks

to Curb Unions," *New York Times*, November 24, 1981.
35. Moore, "The Invincible Mrs. Thatcher."
36. Pan Pylas, "Britain's EU Journey: When Thatcher Turned All Euroskeptic," AP, January 23, 2020, https://apnews.com/article/brexit-business-international-news-europe-margaret-thatcher-64855d1ff67454443db5132bdfb22ea6.
37. Moore, "The Invincible Mrs. Thatcher."
38. Moore, *Margaret Thatcher*, 221.
39. R. W. Apple Jr., "Mrs. Thatcher's Stern Will Is Respected If Not Yet Loved," *New York Times*, October 14, 1979.
40. Moore, "The Invincible Mrs. Thatcher."
41. Moore, *Margaret Thatcher*, 313.
42. Ibid., 350.
43. Ibid., 329.
44. Ibid., 275.
45. Ibid., 296.

Chapter 2: Jeane Kirkpatrick
1. Allen Gerson, *The Kirkpatrick Mission* (New York: The Free Press, 1991), 111.
2. Ibid., 18–19.
3. Mary Anastasia O'Grady, "Don't Forget the Victims in Castro's Gulag," *Wall Street Journal*, August 22, 2003.
4. "Gulag," History, https://www.history.com/topics/russia/gulag.

5. Jeane Kirkpatrick, *Legitimacy and Force: Politicial and Moral Dimensions* (New Jersey: Transaction Books, 1988), 229.

6. Kathryn Watson, "Nikki Haley Responds to White House Claims: 'I Don't Get Confused," CBS News, April 17, 2018, https://www.cbsnews.com/news/with-all-due -respect-i-dont-get-confused-nikki-haley -says-of-russia-sanctions/.

7. Gerson, *The Kirkpatrick Mission*, 18.

8. "Fighting the 'Zionism Is Racism' Lie: Moynihan's Historic U.N. Speech," UN Watch, November 10, 2015, https://unwatch .org/moynihans-moment-the-historic-1975-u -n-speech-in-response-to-zionism-is-racism/.

9. Michael Dobbs, "The Day Adlai Stevenson Showed 'Em at the U.N.," *Washington Post*, February 5, 2003.

10. Peter Collier, *Political Woman: The Big Little Life of Jeane Kirkpatrick* (New York: Encounter Books, 2012), 168.

11. Gerson, *The Kirkpatrick Mission*, xvi.

12. Thom Patterson, "The Downing of Flight 007: 30 Years Later, a Cold War Tragedy Still Seems Surreal," CNN, August 31, 2013.

13. Ibid.

14. Gerson, *The Kirkpatrick Mission*, 198–199.

15. Ibid.

16. Ibid., 204.

17. William J. Eaton, "Soviet Downing of Flight

007 Recalled—Kremlin Was Silent for 5 Days," *Los Angeles Times*, July 4, 1988.

18. Vasily Gatov, "Eight Years to an Apology: Russia's Reaction to MH17 and KAL007," *Moscow Times*, October 6, 2016.

19. "President Reagan's Address to the Nation on the Soviet Attack on a Korean Airliner (KAL 007)," YouTube video, 16:47, posted by Reagan Foundation, April 23, 2011, https://www.youtube.com/watch?v=9VA 4W1wDMAk.

20. Gerson, *The Kirkpatrick Mission*, 203–205.

21. Ibid., 208–209.

22. "Transcript of Kirkpatrick Address on Korean Airliner to Security Council," *New York Times*, September 7, 1983, https://www .nytimes.com/1983/09/07/world/transcript -of-kirkpatrick-address-on-korean-airliner-to -security-council.html.

23. Gerson, *The Kirkpatrick Mission*, 199.

24. "Transcript," *New York Times*.

25. Ibid.

26. Gerson, *The Kirkpatrick Mission*, xiii.

27. Ibid., 212.

28. Ibid., 212–214; Julie Brossy, "The Soviet Union Vetoed a Security Council Resolution Monday . . . ," UPI, September 12, 1983.

29. Gerson, *The Kirkpatrick Mission*, 212–214.

30. Brossy, "Soviet Union."

31. Gerson, *The Kirkpatrick Mission*, 211.

32. Collier, *Political Woman*, 96–99.
33. " 'Blame America First'—Remarks at the 1984 Republican National Committee—Aug. 20, 1984," Iowa State University, Archives of Women's Political Communication, https://awpc.cattcenter.iastate.edu/2017/03/09/remarks-at-the-1984-rnc-aug-20-1984/.
34. Ibid.
35. "Presidential Ad: 'It's Morning Again in America' Ronald Reagan (R) v Walter Mondale (D)," YouTube video, 1:00, posted by New York Historical Society, https://youtu.be/pUMqic2IcWA.

Chapter 3: Golda Meir

1. Golda Meir, *My Life* (New York: G.P. Putnam's Sons, 1975), 26.
2. Francine Klagsbrun, *Lioness: Golda Meir and the Nation of Israel* (New York: Schocken, 2017), 9.
3. Meir, *My Life*, 13.
4. Ibid., 13, 17–22.
5. Klagsbrun, *Lioness*, 22–23.
6. Meir, *My Life*, 26.
7. Ibid., 28–29.
8. Klagsbrun, *Lioness*, 25.
9. Meir, *My Life*, 38–39.
10. Ibid., 40–41.
11. Ibid., 42–44.

12. Ibid., 44.
13. Ibid., 45–46.
14. Ibid., 56–58.
15. Ibid., 59–60.
16. Ibid., 62–67.
17. Ibid., 71–77.
18. Ibid., 82.
19. Ibid., 87–97.
20. Ibid., 109–113.
21. Ibid., 117–118.
22. Ibid., 130; Klagsbrun, *Lioness*, 124–131.
23. Klagsbrun, *Lioness*, 120.
24. Meir, *My Life*, 115–116.
25. Klagsbrun, *Lioness*, 118.
26. Ibid., 127–131.
27. Ibid., 153–163.
28. Ibid., 173–174.
29. Ibid., 184–189.
30. Ibid., 208.
31. Ibid., 209–210.
32. Ibid., 212.
33. Ibid., 215–216
34. Ibid., 212–214.
35. Meir, *My Life*, 13.
36. Klagsbrun, *Lioness*, 220.
37. Ibid., 226–230.
38. Ibid., 231.
39. Ibid., 231–232.
40. Ibid., 240–241.
41. Ibid., 244–258.

42. Ibid., 292–293.
43. Ibid., 300–302.
44. Ibid., 304–308.
45. Ibid., 312.
46. Ibid., 321–325.
47. Ibid., 228.
48. Ibid., 231.

Chapter 4: Cindy Warmbier
1. Interview with Cindy Warmbier, March 14, 2022.
2. Zachary Cohen and Richard Roth, " 'I Will Not Shut Up,' Haley Tells Palestinian Negotiator," CNN, February 21, 2018, https://www.cnn.com/2018/02/20/politics/haley-un-speech-abbas/index.html.
3. Kelly Allan, "Introducing a Small Business Owner Who Discovered Growth Is a Blessing and a Curse," *Forbes*, September 26, 2015.
4. Interview with Cindy Warmbier, March 14, 2022.
5. Doug Bock Clark, "The Untold Story of Otto Warmbier, American Hostage," *GQ*, July 23, 2018; Hyung-Jin Kim and Rebecca Butts, "Wyoming Grad Arrested in North Korea for 'Hostile Act,' " Associated Press, January 25, 2016.
6. Anna Fifield, "What It's Like to Be an American Held in North Korea," *Washington Post*, March 31, 2016.

7. Clark, "Untold Story"; Interview with Cindy Warmbier, March 14, 2022.

8. Clark, "Untold Story."

9. Ibid.

10. Ibid.

11. Ibid.

12. Ibid.

13. Interview with Cindy Warmbier, March 14, 2022.

14. Clark, "Untold Story."

15. Interview with Cindy Warmbier, March 14, 2022.

16. Will Ripley, "U.S. Student Detained in North Korea Confesses to 'Hostile Act,'" CNN, February 29, 2016, https://www.cnn.com/2016/02/28/asia/north-korea-otto-warmbier/index.html.

17. James Pearson and Jack Kim, "North Korea Says U.S. Student Confessed to Theft of Item with Propaganda Slogan," Reuters, February 28, 2016, https://www.reuters.com/article/us-northkorea-usa-student/north-korea-says-u-s-student-confessed-to-theft-of-item-with-propaganda-slogan-idUSKCN0W2094.

18. Clark, "Untold Story."

19. Choe Sang-Hun and Rick Gladstone, "North Korea Sentences Otto Warmbier, U.S. Student, to 15 Years' Labor," *New York Times*, March 16, 2016.

20. Interview with Cindy Warmbier, March 14, 2022.
21. Clark, "Untold Story."
22. Ibid.
23. Interview with Cindy Warmbier, March 14, 2022.
24. Clark, "Untold Story."
25. Ibid.
26. Jason Kurtz, " 'He Was on His Deathbed When He Came Home to Us'—Otto Warmbier's Father," CNN, September 27, 2017, https://www.cnn.com/2017/09/26/politics/fred-cindy-warmbier-parents-otto-north-korea-brooke-baldwin-cnn-newsroom-cnntv/index.html.
27. Cameron Knight, "Otto Warmbier: Mother Says When He Came Home, He Looked 'Like He'd Seen the Devil. And He Had,' " *Cincinnati Enquirer*, May 3, 2019.
28. Emily Shapiro, "Otto Warmbier Was 'Blind and Deaf' When He Returned to the US from North Korea, Parents Say," ABC News, September 26, 2017, https://abcnews.go.com/US/otto-warmbier-blind-deaf-returned-us-parents/story?id=50099791.
29. Anne Saker, "Five Things We Learned from the Warmbiers' Court Victory over North Korea," *Cincinnati Enquirer*, December 26, 2018.
30. Associated Press, "North Korea Denies

Torture, Says It Is 'Biggest Victim' in Otto Warmbier's Death," *Los Angeles Times*, June 23, 2017.

31. Kurtz, "He Was on His Deathbed When He Came Home to Us."

32. Associated Press, "Otto Warmbier's Parents Speak Out Against North Korea," TribLIVE, September 26, 2017, https://archive.triblive .com/news/otto-warmbiers-parents-speak -out-against-north-korea/.

33. Edith M. Lederer, "Otto Warmbier's Mom Now Speaking Out to Embarrass North Korea," Associated Press, May 3, 2018, https://apnews.com/article/united-nations -donald-trump-us-news-ap-top-news-north -korea-c5cc4637876a45fe8ce0a4b641cf6963.

34. "Cindy Warmbier Calls Diplomacy with North Korea a 'Charade,' " YouTube video, 1:50, posted by CBS Evening News, May 3, 2019, https://youtu.be/22INqxCkW0A.

35. David Nakamura, "Trump Puts North Korea Back on State Sponsors of Terrorism List to Escalate Pressure over Nuclear Weapons," *Washington Post*, November 20, 2017.

36. Conor Finnegan, "Otto Warmbier's Parents Tell North Korea: 'We're Never Going to Let You Forget Our Son,' " ABC News, December 18, 2019, https://abcnews.go.com /Politics/otto-warmbiers-parents-north-korea -forget-son/story?id=67802564.

37. Camila Domonoske, "Otto Warmbier's Parents Sue North Korea, Alleging Torture of Their Son," NPR, April 26, 2018, https://www.npr.org/sections/thetwo-way/2018/04/26/606108086/otto-warmbiers-parents-sue-north-korea-alleging-torture-of-their-son.

38. Susan Svrluga and Rachel Weiner, "Judge Orders North Korea to Pay More Than $500 Million in Damages for Otto Warmbier's Death," *Washington Post*, December 24, 2018.

39. Kim Young-gyo and Eunjung Cho, "Otto Warmbier's Parents Chase North Korean Assets in Eastern Europe," *VOA,* July 10, 2020, https://www.voanews.com/a/usa_otto-warmbiers-parents-chase-north-korean-assets-eastern-europe/6192569.html.

40. Elizabeth Shim, "U.S. Court Orders Disclosure of $23M in North Korea Assets to Warmbiers," UPI, May 12, 2020.

41. "North Korea's Kim Jong-un Faces 'Paradise on Earth' Lawsuit," BBC News, October 14, 2021.

42. Lia Eustachewich, "Human Rights Group Files $28M Suit Against North Korea over Korean War Abductions," *New York Post*, June 25, 2020.

43. "The Otto Warmbier Story: Imprisoned and Left Brain Dead by North Korea," *60 Minutes Australia*, April 1, 2021.

44. Interview with Cindy Warmbier, March 14, 2022.
45. Ibid.
46. Max Boot and Sue Mi Terry, "Opinion: This Ex-Marine Tried to Help North Korean Diplomats Defect. Now He Faces Decades in Prison," *Washington Post*, May 2, 2021.
47. Eric Shawn, "Calls Intensify for Biden Administration to Help Save Former Marine's Life," Fox News, June 5, 2021, https://www.foxnews.com/politics/biden -administration-help-save-us-marine.

Chapter 5: Nadia Murad

1. "Ambassador Nikki Haley Meets with Nadia Murad and Amal Clooney," United States Mission to the United Nations, March 9, 2017, https://usun.usmission.gov /ambassador-nikki-haley-meets-with-nadia -murad-and-amal-clooney/.
2. Jennifer Peltz, "UN Votes to Help Iraq Collect Evidence Against Islamic State," Associated Press, September 21, 2017, https://apnews.com/article/6bfacfeedbae 43f3b806b754b574a229.
3. Nadia Murad, *The Last Girl: My Story of Captivity, and My Fight Against the Islamic State* (New York: Tim Duggan Books, 2017), 306.
4. "Remarks at the U.S. Holocaust Memorial

Museum Program 'Our Walls Bear Witness: South Sudan—Where Do We Go From Here?,'" United States Mission to the United Nations, November 15, 2017, https://usun .usmission.gov/remarks-at-the-u-s-holocaust -memorial-museum-program-our-walls-bear -witness-south-sudan-where-do-we-go-from -here/.

5. *On Her Shoulders*, directed by Alexandria Bombach (Los Angeles, CA: RYOT Films, 2018).
6. "About the Genocide," Nadia's Initiative, https://www.nadiasinitiative.org/the-genocide.
7. Murad, *The Last Girl,* 10.
8. Ibid., 22–23.
9. *On Her Shoulders* (2018); Murad, *The Last Girl*, 19–24.
10. Murad, *The Last Girl*, 52–53.
11. Ibid., 63–64.
12. Ibid., 56, 61.
13. Ibid., 61, 68–70.
14. Ibid., 67, 75.
15. Ibid., 82–103.
16. Ibid., 103–107.
17. Ibid., 112–114.
18. Ibid., 118–119.
19. Ibid., 122.
20. Ibid., 136–137.
21. Ibid., 146.
22. Ibid., 141–151.

23. Ibid., 161.
24. Ibid., 131.
25. Ibid.
26. Ibid., 167.
27. Ibid., 173–175.
28. Ibid., 185.
29. Ibid., 199–209.
30. Ibid., 209–211.
31. Ibid., 213–214.
32. Ibid., 217–250.
33. Ibid., 280–281.
34. Ibid., 283–284.
35. Ibid., 286.
36. Ibid., 289.
37. Ibid., 177.
38. Ibid., 300.
39. Ibid., 302.
40. Ibid., 302–303.
41. Ibid.
42. Ibid., 303.
43. Ibid., 305–306.
44. Ibid., 300.
45. *On Her Shoulders* (2018).
46. Scott Pelley, "Nadia Murad's Vow to Take ISIS to Court, and Her Heartbreaking Return Home," CBS News, October 4, 2020, https://www.cbsnews.com/news/nobel-peace-prize-recipient-nadia-murad-amal-clooney-isis-court-60-minutes-2020–10–04/.
47. "ISIL Crimes Against Yazidis Constitute

Genocide, UN Investigation Team Finds," UN News, May 10, 2021, https://news.un.org/en/story/2021/05/1091662.

48. "Statement by Nadia Murad and Amal Clooney on First ISIS Conviction for Genocide," Nadia's Initiative, November 30, 2021, https://www.nadiasinitiative.org/news/nadia-murad-and-amal-clooney-joint-statement-of-genocide-conviction-of-isis-perpetrator.

49. "Human Trafficking Survivor Nadia Murad Named UNODC Goodwill Ambassador," United Nations, Office on Drugs and Crime, September 16, 2016, https://www.unodc.org/unodc/en/frontpage/2016/September/human-trafficking-survivor-nadia-murad-named-unodc-goodwill-ambassador.html.

50. "Nadia Murad—Facts," Nobel Prize, https://www.nobelprize.org/prizes/peace/2018/murad/facts/.

51. "Timeline: The Rise, Spread, and Fall of the Islamic State," Wilson Center, October 28, 2019, https://www.wilsoncenter.org/article/timeline-the-rise-spread-and-fall-the-islamic-state.

52. "Nobel Peace Prize Winner Nadia Murad on Taking ISIS to Court," Georgetown Institute for Women, Peace and Security, https://giwps.georgetown.edu/nobel-peace-prize-winner-nadia-murad-on-taking-isis-to-court/.

53. "Women's Empowerment," Nadia's Initiative,

https://www.nadiasinitiative.org/womens
-empowerment.

54. "Pakiza's Story: Empowerment through Entrepreneurship," Nadia's Initiative, March 25, 2022, https://www.nadiasinitiative.org /news/pakizas-story-empowerment-through -entrepreneurship.

55. "About the Genocide," Nadia's Initiative.

Chapter 6: Virginia Walden Ford

1. "Ramp Up Rural Education," *Post and Courier*, May 27, 2014.

2. "A Lifetime of Fighting for Education for All," *Catalyst*, Summer 2020, https://www .bushcenter.org/catalyst/still-leaving-them -behind/virginia-walden-ford-a-lifetime -fighting-for-education.html.

3. "State of the State Address 2014," YouTube video, 1:18:35, posted by South Carolina ETV, January 22, 2014, https://youtu.be/5C _TpW4kDw0.

4. "Meet Virginia Walden Ford," Virginia Walden Ford, https://www.virginiawalden ford.com/about-virginia/.

5. "Miss Virginia: Movie Discussion with Virginia Walden Ford," YouTube video, 23:25, posted by UOFLCOB, November 16, 2021, https://youtu.be/Gy8dan2WEew; "The Movie 'Miss Virginia' Powerfully Dramatizes the Urgent Need for School

Choice," YouTube video, 10:25, posted by ReasonTV, October 18, 2019, https://you tu.be/ehCjqBTChzs.

6. Virginia Walden Ford, *School Choice: A Legacy to Keep* (New York: Beaufort Books, 2019), 11–12.

7. "What Prejudice Taught Me About Advocacy," Virginia Walden Ford, July 23, 2019, https://www.virginiawaldenford .com/2019/07/23/what-prejudice-taught-me -about-advocacy/

8. Ford, *School Choice*, 53–55.

9. "Virginia Walden Ford—The Struggle for an Education—May 2021," YouTube video, 1:08:22, posted by Northwood University Presents, May 16, 2021, https://youtu.be /FD92QzyEr3I.

10. Ford, *School Choice*, 56.

11. Ibid., 56, 81.

12. "A Lifetime of Fighting," *Catalyst*.

13. "A Conversation with Virginia Walden Ford," YouTube video, 3:12, posted by the Bush Center, August 17, 2000, https://you tu.be/E3tjowS49eM.

14. Ford, *School Choice*, 59–73; "A Lifetime of Fighting," *Catalyst*.

15. Ford, *School Choice*, 63, 71.

16. Ibid., 67–70.

17. Ibid., 59.

18. Ibid., 79.

19. Ibid., 79–82.
20. Benjamin D. Stafford, *Choice Leadership* (Midland, MI: Mackinac Center for Public Policy, 2007), https://www.mackinac.org /archives/2007/s2007–15.pdf.
21. "A Lifetime of Fighting," *Catalyst.*
22. "How a Mother Became a School Choice Champion," Independent Women's Forum, https://www.iwf.org/people/virginia-walden -ford/.
23. Stafford, *Choice Leadership.*
24. Ford, *School Choice*, 113, 119–120.
25. "Republican Pushes Bill for Vouchers," *Washington Times*, February 12, 2003.
26. "Coalition Letter to the House Urging Opposition to the School Voucher Program for the District of Columbia," ACLU, September 5, 2003, https://www.aclu.org /letter/coalition-letter-house-urging -opposition-school-voucher-program-district -columbia.
27. Ford, *School Choice*, 134.
28. Stafford, *Choice Leadership.*
29. Ibid.
30. "School Choice Champion," Independent Women's Forum.
31. Anthony A. Williams, Kevin P. Chavous, and Peggy Cooper Cafritz, "Washington's Children Deserve More Choices," *Washington Post*, September 3, 2003.

32. Spencer S. Hsu, "How Vouchers Came to D.C.," *Education Next* 4, no. 4 (Fall 2004).
33. "D.C. Becomes School Voucher Battleground," CNN, June 12, 2003.
34. "House Passes D.C. School Voucher Plan in 209–208 Revote," Baptist Press, September 10, 2003, http://m.bpnews.net/16645/house-passes-dc-school-voucher-plan-in-209208-revote.
35. "Roll Call 490 | Bill Number: H. R. 2765," U.S. House of Representative, September 9, 2003, https://clerk.house.gov/Votes/2003490.
36. "House Passes D.C. School Voucher Plan in 209–208 Revote," Baptist Press; George Will, "Vouching for Children," *Washington Post*, September 14, 2003.
37. Ford, *School Choice*, 138; Spencer S. Hsu, "Senate Backs Off D.C. School Voucher," *Washington Post*, October 1, 2003.
38. "President Bush Signs Voucher Legislation," Council for American Private Education, February 2004.
39. Rod Paige, "A Time for Choice," Heritage Foundation, February 2, 2004, https://www.heritage.org/education/report/time-choice.
40. Ford, *School Choice*, 144–145.
41. Ibid., 144–145.
42. Ibid., 146–147.
43. Ibid., 151, 155–156.
44. Ibid., 157.

45. Ibid., 160–161.
46. Gary Emerling, "Vouchers in D.C. to Get Reprieve," *Washington Times*, May 7, 2009.
47. Ford, *School Choice*, 165–170.
48. Ibid., 170–171.
49. Ibid., 172.
50. "About Serving Our Children," Serving Our Children, https://servingourchildrendc.org/about-us/.

Chapter 7: Claudette Colvin

1. George Will, "As GOP Diversifies, South Carolina Is Rising," *Washington Post*, September 9, 2010, https://www.washingtonpost.com/wp-dyn/content/article/2010/09/08/AR2010090805706.html?hpid=opinionsbox1.
2. Justin Worland, "This Is Why South Carolina Raised the Confederate Flag in the First Place," *Time*, June 22, 2015.
3. Margot Adler, "Before Rosa Parks, There Was Claudette Colvin," NPR, March 15, 2009, https://www.npr.org/2009/03/15/101719889/before-rosa-parks-there-was-claudette-colvin.
4. "Inauguration of Jefferson Davis," *Encyclopedia of Alabama*, http://encyclopediaofalabama.org/article/m-3598.
5. Phillip Hoose, *Claudette Colvin: Twice Towards Justice* (New York: Farrar, Straus and Giroux, 2009), 13.

6. Ibid., 21.
7. Ibid., 16–17.
8. Ibid., 12.
9. Ibid., 22.
10. Ibid.
11. Ibid., 25–26.
12. Ibid., 27.
13. Ibid., 7.
14. Ibid.
15. Ibid.
16. Ibid., 29.
17. Ibid., 30.
18. Great Big Story, "Claudette Colvin: The Original Rosa Parks," YouTube, https://www.youtube.com/watch?v=V3NvXzFOb6w&t=35s.
19. Hoose, *Claudette Colvin*, 30.
20. Ibid., 30–32.
21. Ibid., 32.
22. Ibid.
23. Ibid., 34.
24. Oliver Laughland, "Claudette Colvin: The Woman Who Refused to Give Up Her Bus Seat—Nine Months Before Rosa Parks," *The Guardian*, February 25, 2021, https://www.theguardian.com/society/2021/feb/25/claudette-colvin-the-woman-who-refused-to-give-up-her-bus-seat-nine-months-before-rosa-parks.
25. Hoose, *Claudette Colvin*, 34.

26. Ibid., 34–35.
27. Ibid., 37–40.
28. Ibid., 40–43.
29. Ibid., 42–43.
30. Ibid., 44–45.
31. Ibid., 47.
32. Ibid., 47–48.
33. Ibid., 58–59.
34. Jo Ann Gibson Robinson, *The Montgomery Bus Boycott and the Women Who Started It: The Memoir of Jo Ann Gibson Robinson* (Knoxville, TN: The University of Tennessee Press, 1987), 45–46, 58.
35. Ibid., 40, 91–94.
36. Hoose, *Claudette Colvin*, 69–71.
37. Ibid., 71.
38. Ibid., 72–73.
39. Ibid., 73–74.
40. Ibid., 80–81; Robinson, *The Montgomery Bus Boycott and the Women Who Started It*, 149.
41. Hoose, *Claudette Colvin*, 85–88.
42. Ibid., 91–92.
43. Ibid., 91–94.
44. Ibid., 98, 102.
45. Ibid., 38–39; Robinson, *The Montgomery Bus Boycott and the Women Who Started It*, 135.
46. Hoose, *Claudette Colvin*, 58–59.
47. Ibid., 103.

48. Michele L. Norris, "Opinion: Before Rosa Parks, Claudette Colvin Refused to Give Up Her Seat on a Bus. She's Still on Probation," *Washington Post*, October 26, 2021; Hoose, *Claudette Colvin*, 49.

49. Jay Reeves, Associated Press, "Civil Rights Pioneer Seeks Expungement of '55 Arrest Record," ABC News, October 26, 2021, https://abcnews.go.com/US/wireStory/civil -rights-pioneer-seeks-expungement-55-arrest -record-80784675.

Chapter 8: Virginia Hall

1. Somini Sengupta, "Nikki Haley Puts U.N. on Notice: U.S. Is 'Taking Names,'" *New York Times*, January 27, 2017.

2. Sonia Purnell, *A Woman of No Importance: The Untold Story of the American Spy Who Helped Win World War II* (New York: Viking, 2019), 7.

3. Ibid., 164–165.

4. Ibid., 166.

5. Ibid., 7–8.

6. Ibid., 8–9.

7. Carl Schoettler, "A Cloak-and-Dagger Life Is Exposed for All to See," *Baltimore Sun*, November 25, 2004.

8. Purnell, *A Woman of No Importance*, 11–12.

9. Ibid., 12–13.

10. Judith L. Pearson, *The Wolves at the Door:*

The True Story of America's Greatest Female Spy (New York: Diversion Books, 2005), 15–17.

11. Ibid., 18–19; Purnell, *A Woman of No Importance*, 15–16.
12. Purnell, *A Woman of No Importance*, 16–19.
13. Pearson, *The Wolves at the Door*, 35–37.
14. Purnell, *A Woman of No Importance*, 22–25.
15. Ibid., 28–38.
16. Ibid., 38–40.
17. Ibid., 45, 59–66.
18. Ibid., 71–72.
19. Ibid., 81–82.
20. Ibid., 82–90.
21. Ibid., 92–94.
22. Ibid., 115–119.
23. Ibid., 121–124.
24. Ibid., 124–126.
25. Ibid., 127, 141.
26. Ibid., 144–152.
27. Ibid., 153–159.
28. Ibid., 166.
29. Ibid., 162, 171–178.
30. Ibid., 181–182.
31. Ibid., 190–191.
32. Ibid., 201.
33. Ibid., 196–199; Pearson, *The Wolves at the Door*, 6–8.
34. Purnell, *A Woman of No Importance*, 199–202.

35. Ibid., 206–211, 218–219.
36. Ibid., 219–223.
37. Ibid., 253–254.
38. Ibid., 266.
39. Ibid., 279, 297–298.

Chapter 9: Wilma Rudolph

1. "Wilma Rudolph's Incredible Career | Olympic Records," YouTube video, 2:49, posted by Olympics, September 26, 2014, https://www.youtube.com/watch?v=JqI8NyZtCmo.
2. Maureen M. Smith, *Wilma Rudolph: A Biography* (Westport, CT: Greenwood, 2006), 1.
3. Ibid., 1–2.
4. Wilma Rudolph, *Wilma* (New York: First Signet Printing, 1977), 29.
5. Ibid., 30.
6. Ibid., 30–31; Smith, *Wilma Rudolph*, 2–3.
7. Frank Litsky, "Wilma Rudolph, Star of the 1960 Olympics, Dies at 54," *New York Times*, November 13, 1994.
8. Rudolph, *Wilma*, 31–32, 38; Smith, *Wilma Rudolph*, 4.
9. Smith, *Wilma Rudolph*, 2–3.
10. Ira Berkow, "Forever the Regal Champion," *New York Times*, November 13, 1994.
11. Smith, *Wilma Rudolph*, 4.
12. Ibid., 7–8.
13. Rudolph, *Wilma*, 43–44.

14. Smith, *Wilma Rudolph*, 9–10; Rudolph, *Wilma*, 45.
15. Smith, *Wilma Rudolph*, 11–12.
16. Rudolph, *Wilma*, 64–66.
17. Smith, *Wilma Rudolph*, 13.
18. Ibid., 15–19.
19. Ibid., 23–25.
20. Ibid., 37.
21. Rudolph, *Wilma*, 96–98.
22. David Maraniss, *Rome 1960: The Summer Olympics That Changed the World* (New York: Simon & Schuster, 2008), 56.
23. Ibid., 142–143.
24. Ibid., 238, 252.
25. Ibid., 267.
26. Ibid., 267–268.
27. Ibid., 268, 319–321.
28. Ibid., 196.
29. Rudolph, *Wilma*, 70–71.
30. Maraniss, *Rome 1960*, 321–322.
31. Ibid., 393.
32. Rudolph, *Wilma*, 74–75.
33. Maraniss, *Rome 1960*, 394–395.
34. Ibid., 484.
35. Ibid., 484–485.
36. Ibid., 486.
37. Ibid., 47.
38. James Morris, "Trial of U-2 Spy Plane Pilot Gary Powers Begins—Archive, 1960," *Guardian*, August 18, 2020.
39. Maraniss, *Rome 1960*, 47–48.

Chapter 10: Amelia Earhart

1. "Quotes," Amelia Earhart, https://amelia earhart.com/quotes/.
2. Susan Butler, *East to the Dawn: The Life of Amelia Earhart* (Boston: Da Capo, 1997), 144.
3. Ibid.
4. "Amelia Earhart," Smithsonian Air and Space Museum, https://airandspace.si.edu /amelia-earhart.
5. Keith O'Brien, *Fly Girls* (Boston: Houghton Mifflin Harcourt, 2018), Kindle edition, location 995 of 7272.
6. Butler, *East to the Dawn*, 152.
7. O'Brien, *Fly Girls*, location 1033, 1081 of 7272.
8. Ibid., location 1073–1106 of 7272.
9. Ibid., location 1113–1146 of 7272.
10. Ibid., location 1135–1154 of 7272.
11. Ibid., location 1162–1187 of 7272.
12. Ibid., location 1187 of 7272.
13. Ibid., location 1187–1204 of 7272.
14. Ibid., location 1212 of 7272.
15. Ibid., location 1341–1461 of 7272.
16. Ibid., location 1461 of 7272.
17. Ibid., location 1461–1478 of 7272.
18. Ibid., location 1478–1485 of 7272.
19. Ibid., location 1584–1602 of 7272.
20. Ibid., location 1626–1634 of 7272.
21. Butler, *East to the Dawn*, 230–231; Mary S.

Lovell, *The Sound of Wings* (New York: St. Martin's, 1989), 148–150.

22. O'Brien, *Fly Girls*, location 1721–1729 of 7272.
23. Ibid., location 1851–1867 of 7272.
24. Ibid., location 1739–1747 of 7272.
25. Butler, *East to the Dawn*, 232.
26. "The Ninety-Nines from 1929 to 1989," Ninety-Nines, https://www.ninety-nines.org /sixty-years.htm; O'Brien, *Fly Girls*, location 1923–1931, 2573 of 7272.
27. O'Brien, *Fly Girls*, location 2334–2357 of 7272.
28. Ibid., location 2534–2542 of 7272.
29. Ibid., location 2573–2613 of 7272.
30. Ibid., location 2621 of 7272.
31. Ibid., location 2893–2973 of 7272.
32. Butler, *East to the Dawn*, 286.
33. O'Brien, *Fly Girls*, location 2991–3015 of 7272.
34. Ibid., location 3040–3047 of 7272.
35. Butler, *East to the Dawn*, 240.
36. Amelia Earhart, *The Fun of It* (London: Arcturus, 2020), Kindle edition, location 1458–1471 of 2219.
37. Butler, *East to the Dawn*, 308–309.
38. O'Brien, *Fly Girls*, location 3778–3783 of 7272.
39. Butler, *East to the Dawn*, 309–312.
40. O'Brien, *Fly Girls*, location 3454–3470 of 7272.

41. Earhart, *The Fun of It*, location 1416.
42. Butler, *East to the Dawn*, 324–327, 334.
43. O'Brien, *Fly Girls*, location 3501 of 7272; Butler, *East to the Dawn*, 341.
44. Butler, *East to the Dawn,* 341–347.
45. O'Brien, *Fly Girls*, location 4180–4192 of 7272.
46. Ibid., location 4196 of 7272.
47. Ibid., location 4200 of 7272; Butler, *East to the Dawn*, 354.
48. O'Brien, *Fly Girls*, location 4241–4297 of 7272.

Center Point Large Print
600 Brooks Road / PO Box 1
Thorndike, ME 04986-0001 USA

(207) 568-3717

US & Canada:
1 800 929-9108
www.centerpointlargeprint.com